The Essential Skills of Wilderness Survival

"Easy. Practical. Efficient. This is one of the rare survival guides that actually leaves the reader immediately more competent with just a few minutes of casual perusal. The concepts are superbly clear, the layout is easily navigated, and each principle is supported with crisp, well-planned photography. For those wanting to be better prepared and feel more confident on any excursion, this book is a must have. The inviting, engaging approach makes it just as beneficial for curious youngsters as it is for knowledge hungry, detail-oriented adults. Get a copy, read it, and leave it out for guests, kids, and neighbors. It could save lives."

—Casey McFarland, wildlife biologist, Senior Tracker and Evaluator, co-author of three field guides including the updated *Peterson Field Guide to North American Bird Nests*

"Everyone needs to know core survival principles and techniques. In **The Essential Skills of Wilderness Survival**, Jason Knight distills these skills and concepts into a format that ensures success. He couples this with full-color diagrams and photos to ensure the reader will gain the confidence and know-how to be prepared for survival emergencies. This book provides valuable guidance for new and experienced outdoor enthusiasts alike."

—Nicole Apelian, Ph.D., wilderness skills instructor, and author of four books including *The Forager's Guide to Wild Foods: Edible Plants, Lichens, Mushrooms, and Seaweeds*

"Having taught survival skills for nearly two decades, I strongly believe that the skills described in this book are not simply "wilderness skills", but are in fact critical life skills that every one of us should possess. The ability to take care of one's own needs in critical situations is not only essential, but also liberating and empowering. This book is a great resource on your journey of self-reliance and self-discovery and one worth having in your library."

—Dave Scott, survival and wildlife tracking expert, founder of Earth Native Wilderness School

"Whether you are looking to deepen your connection to the natural world or prepare for when things go wrong, Jason has captured the fundamentals of wilderness survival in an easy to read and well-organized book that is chock full of useful tips. This book will certainly be added to the cannon of required and suggested readings for all of our school's staff and participants."

—Scott Brinton, executive director of CedarRoot Folk School

"**The Essential Skills of Wilderness Survival** contains lifesaving information that's vital to have in a book, since the internet might not be there in a survival situation. There are few wilderness teachers who know their stuff as well as Jason Knight. He's written a complete guide that's 100% trustworthy. This is a refreshing book that tells you exactly what you need to know and leaves out the filler. I am positive that **The Essential Skills of Wilderness Survival** will be the most important book that you ever own."

—John Gallagher, herbalist, educator, and cofounder of LearningHerbs.com

"I spend a good deal of time in some wild country, often miles from the nearest trail or road. Whether tracking, hunting or running I always have a question in the back of my mind: Am I ready if I cannot make it back? Jason's book prepares you to answer that question. This book will leave you with a practical understanding of what fundamentals you need to prioritize and execute should that lingering question become a reality. This knowledge is spoken by someone who has not only mastered these skills but also mastered how to present them as an educator."

—Brian McConnell, wildlife tracker,
Master Hunter and mentor, backcountry ultrarunner

"Having taught thousands of students and read many survival guides over the years, this book does a great job introducing people to the world of survival. This guide invites readers in and provides them with the knowledge to gain new skills and build on existing experience increasing their knowledge and confidence to venture further into the wilderness safely."

—Mike Pewtherer, author of *Wilderness Survival Handbook*
and founder of Woodland Ways

"Jason's scientific and methodical approach to wilderness survival, combined with his helpful personal stories and examples, allow the reader to solidly grasp the basics of wilderness survival, so that they can take what they've learned and improvise depending upon their unique situation. This sets Jason's approach apart from others in his field. That's so important, because each survival situation, natural disaster or even backyard party have their own unique set of factors that need to be assessed."

—Kristi Dranginis, author of *Identify Any Bird Anywhere* and founder of BirdMentor.com

"Wherever you are on the journey of connecting to the earth, reading **The Essential Skills of Wilderness Survival** will build a solid foundation for lifelong learning in how to take care of yourself outdoors."

—Carleigh Fairchild, survival consultant, participant on the History Channel's survival show *Alone*, and creator of the "Connecting with Place" Series

"Jason Knight has created a distilled and efficient survival book with no BS. A great book for those who want to develop a solid survival foundation and learn from someone who has lived what he's teaching."

—David Moskowitz, biologist, photographer, educator, and author of three books: *Caribou Rainforest, Wildlife of the Pacific Northwest,* and *Wolves in the Land of Salmon*

"Jason Knight has put together an incredibly helpful and accessible guide to wilderness survival. Perfect for beginners, as well as seasoned veterans, **The Essential Skills of Wilderness Survival** is a must have for any survival enthusiast's bookshelf. I highly recommend it."

—Nate Summers, survival skills instructor and author of *Awakening Fire: The Essential Guide*

"As you might expect from someone with long experience both doing and teaching, someone also articulate and well-versed, Jason Knight presents brief and crystal-clear guidance to woodsfolk of all skill levels who wish to deepen their practice of essential bushcraft. Here you find the surest path through a rapidly changing environment."

—Nate Harvey, Senior Tracker and CyberTracker Evaluator, founder of TrackersTrail.com

"What a visually rich, concise and well-organized concentration of knowledge Jason has compiled from his years of experience! Filled with straight forward, easy to remember guidelines with accurate and clear, step-by-step visuals, this is ideal for those just starting out, or the already experienced looking for new tips and skills. Highly recommend."

—Heidi Bohan, ethnobotany educator and author of
The People of Cascadia

"This is an excellent resource for those intending to be comfortable in the wilderness for any amount of time. If everyone took these contents to heart, we would have fewer searches for missing persons, and more outings completed successfully."

—Rob Speiden, Search and Rescue Instructor,
professional tracker, and author of
Foundations for Awareness, Signcutting, and Tracking

"This guide is a must-read for anyone wanting to build their self-sufficiency skills, whether or not they spend time in the wilderness. Jason Knight's approach to teaching and learning survival makes this knowledge very accessible."

—Julie Stonefelt, Park Ranger and cofounder of Wild Homestead Living

"This easy-to-read book provides you with simple to use and fun to practice survival skills. If practiced, these skills will create calmness, and calmness is the most powerful survival tool to have."

—Adriaan Louw, Master Tracker and CyberTracker Evaluator,
and co-author of *Practical Tracking*

"I have worked with Jason Knight for many years and can attest first-hand to his expert survival and tracking skills. In this book Jason offers a comprehensive survival guide containing clearly written and pictured how-tos for all the skills one needs to tackle wilderness, or any other unexpected challenges, and come out alive."

—Dan Stueber, flintknapping instructor and founder of
Thunderstones Lithic Consulting

"What makes a great survival book? Practical, no-nonsense information. You'll find that with Jason's clear expertise and instruction. **The Essential Skills of Wilderness Survival** is an essential survival guide for everyone."

—Tony Deis, founder of Trackers Earth outdoor programs

"**The Essential Skills of Wilderness Survival** contains excellent descriptions and photographs of the core skills and techniques that will keep you alive when the unexpected occurs in an outdoor setting. Knight's decades of experience practicing and teaching modern survival and earth-based nature skills, the clear-concise format of the book, and the quality color photographs provide the reader with detailed instructions on how to practice for an emergency survival situation."

—Preston Taylor, biologist, Senior Tracker and CyberTracker Evaluator, and author of *Tracking the American Black Bear*

"**The Essential Skills of Wilderness Survival** is just that—essential knowledge for those who enjoy spending time outdoors in the backcountry. This concise, thorough guide provides the framework for those beginning on their journey of preparedness and self-reliance."

—Chrissy Roberts, owner and director of Quiet Heart Wilderness School

"Jason Knight has the knowledge we all need and he's done an amazing job placing it in this book that is full of practical wisdom. If I were you, I'd start reading it right away."

—Victor Wooten, naturalist, teacher, Grammy-winning bassist, founder of VixCamps Center for Music and Nature, and author of *The Music Lesson*

"A beautifully illustrated and masterfully organized guide that simplifies Jason's decades of experience teaching the complex art of wilderness survival into a wonderfully accessible format. Whether you're a seasoned nature enthusiast or new to the outdoors, this book will be an invaluable companion!"

—Jonah Evans, Nongame and Rare Species Program Leader at Texas Parks and Wildlife; and founder of NatureTracking.com

Before you dive in, be sure to receive the bonus survival skills resources created especially for this book by visiting:

https://www.wildernesscollege.com/survival-book-bonuses.html

ALSO AVAILABLE FROM
ALDERLEAF WILDERNESS COLLEGE

The Essential Wilderness Survival Skills Online Course is the perfect companion to this book! Alderleaf instructors bring *The Essential Skills of Wilderness Survival* to life by demonstrating each of the techniques presented, showing you how you can further develop your survival knowledge.

Learn more at:
https://www.wildernesscollege.com/essential-wilderness-survival-skills.html

Additionally, the Alderleaf website, www.WildernessCollege.com, has many wilderness skills resources including videos, classes, and hundreds of how-to articles.

ALDERLEAF WILDERNESS COLLEGE

The Essential Skills of

WILDERNESS SURVIVAL

A GUIDE TO SHELTER, WATER, FIRE, FOOD, NAVIGATION, AND SURVIVAL KITS

JASON KNIGHT

ALDERLEAF
PRESS

DISCLAIMER

The survival skills and associated information in this book have been researched and tested with much effort to ensure their accuracy. They are for use in emergency situations where safety is at risk. Accordingly, the authors and publishers cannot assume responsibility for any injuries, damages, losses, prosecutions, or proceedings brought or instituted against any person or body as a result of any use or misuse as a result of following this information. The authors and publishers also assume no responsibility for any omissions or errors and make no warranty that the information is appropriate for every situation, individual, or purpose. Before practicing these survival skills, be sure you are aware of your own limitations and have adequately researched all applicable risks. In addition, while practicing wilderness survival, please be respectful of private property rights of landowners and of laws that protect natural resources and plant and animal species.

The Essential Skills of Wilderness Survival:
A Guide to Shelter, Water, Fire, Food, Navigation, and Survival Kits
Copyright © 2022 by Jason Knight

All rights reserved. This book or any portion thereof may not be reproduced or used in any manner whatsoever without the express written permission of the publisher, except for the use of brief quotations in a book review.

Printed in the United States of America

Alderleaf Press

LCCN: 2022902660
ISBN: 979-8-9856918-0-1

*To the thousands of Alderleaf students
who have inspired me with their excitement
and enthusiasm for wilderness skills.*

Table of Contents

Preface

It has been amazing to see how much the field of wilderness survival has changed over the last twenty-five years.

Today, we have far better technology than in the recent past to make our lives safer in the outdoors: GPS, smartphones, internet resources like Google Maps, and many others. However, at the same time, there's been a tremendous uptick in the frequency of folks finding themselves in dire survival situations and in the number of lost person searches both in the wilderness and during natural disasters. This is likely due to these new tools providing a false sense of security. For example, a cell phone can easily run out of battery power, be out of cell signal range, become broken, lost, or forgotten. Without a map and compass (and the know-how to use them) and other survival skills to fall back on, countless individuals become lost, and unfortunately, many perish each year.

On a positive note, having an interest in outdoor survival skills has gone from being looked upon as a strange fringe activity to being seen as a mainstream hobby thanks to numerous popular survival TV shows and movies. It's fantastic that so many folks are getting tuned-in to how valuable and amazing wilderness skills are. Unfortunately, the very things that make a lot of survival shows so popular (the overly dramatic depictions) are often poor survival advice. For example, it's never a good idea to jump off a cliff into a raging river at night or to consume rotting meat when trying to make it out alive. What makes captivating TV isn't necessarily good survival advice.

Finally, twenty-five years ago there was only a handful of survival websites. Now there are thousands. Just go to YouTube.com and search *survival* and you'll find a myriad of videos. And while it is truly awesome to see so much being shared, it can lead to information overload; anyone and everyone can put up a website, upload a video, write a blog, and share a post. There are literally millions of random bits of survival-related information circulating at any given moment. Unfortunately, it can be near impossible to parse out accurate, quality information and then organize it into a sound approach.

This is where *The Essential Skills of Wilderness Survival* comes in. What you'll find in the coming pages is a tried, true, and tested approach to each of the core priorities that must be addressed in wilderness survival situations. It is a cohesive system for taking care of the most pressing survival needs both with and without modern gear. And, it covers the essentials to survival in a concise format. An in-depth reading of *The Essential Skills of Wilderness Survival,* and practice of the skills covered, will reward you with a clear understanding of how to handle wilderness survival emergencies.

The techniques taught in *The Essential Skills of Wilderness Survival* are not just for surviving in the woods. When the power goes out, or when the next hurricane, flood, or earthquake strikes, many of these same techniques can come into play. For example, during the aftermath of hurricanes Irma and Maria in Puerto Rico there were reports of many deaths from drinking leptospirosis-contaminated water. A basic knowledge of survival water purification could have prevented those deaths. The bottom line is that wilderness survival skills are possibly the lowest cost/highest value backup insurance plan for survival situations from domestic and civil emergencies to natural disasters, not just in the deep backcountry.

How to Use This Book

I highly recommend you first read this book from beginning to end. The introduction and first chapter give you the context and an overview of the book to understand the connections between all of the specific skills presented in the middle chapters. The afterword will review key concepts and suggest where to go next in your survival skills journey. Once you've read the book front to back, you can return to specific chapters to use them as a guide for making your first shelter or bow drill fire or for guidance with any of the other skills presented. You'll then be able to tackle those unexpected survival challenges when they arise. And if you wish, you can develop your skills further through the supplemental resources listed in the back of this book.

Introduction

Maybe you are a hiker who wants to know what to do if you get lost. Or maybe you have watched tragic news unfold during a natural disaster and decided you want to know how to take care of yourself and others if you find yourself in such a situation. Or maybe you have been inspired by survival stories you've read and want to learn more. And maybe none of these describe you and the reasons for your interest in survival preparedness.

Regardless, wilderness survival skills are not just for outdoor enthusiasts—they are for everyone. Mastering these skills leads to an unparalleled sense of security, a deepened connection to nature, and a closer relationship to our ancestors and how they once lived as hunter-gatherers. Survival skills are the ultimate backup insurance plan if all else fails and could one day save your life and the lives of those around you.

You will find, within the pages of this book, a world that will transform your idea of *living* for the rest of your life. Once you understand which plants can be eaten, what trees can be turned into a bow drill fire kit or provide the insulation you need to survive a cold night, a forest that may now appear as a wall of green will become a *community of survival allies*. As you continue to learn about the amazing resources of the natural world, you will also discover a stewardship ethic that assures that there will be plenty of wilderness for future generations to enjoy.

This book covers core survival skills needed for common survival emergencies, explained at the depth needed for readers to go out and implement them. Many books present brief explanations of hundreds of outdoor skills. While those books are often inspirational and make great coffee table books, there often isn't enough detail on the survival essentials. Inside this book you will find detailed and easy to follow instructions on how to make an effective shelter, purify water, start a fire, find food, and other essentials. The book also focuses on the techniques most applicable to real survival situations rather than on long-term intentional wilderness living skills. With that said, these core skills are the *key foundations* for diving deeper into primitive living skills.

Every year people find themselves in survival emergencies, and unfortunately, many perish in circumstances that could have been easily remedied by rudimentary wilderness know-how. As you go through this book, you will come to understand your survival priorities and how to address each of them with and without the aid of equipment. By the end, and with some practice, you will become better prepared to take care of yourself and others in survival emergencies in the wilderness or at home. Let's get started!

CHAPTER 1

Core Survival Concepts

D ecades ago, before I started learning about wilderness survival, I really didn't know how hazardous it could be to venture into mountainous terrain without survival skills. One warm summer day, a friend and I decided to hike to the top of Mount Adams, one of the tallest mountains in New England. We got up early, drove up north into New Hampshire from Rockport, Massachusetts, and parked by the trailhead next to a country store.

It was a beautiful sunny morning. I distinctly remember a couple of bearded oldtimers at the store warning us, "You boys better turn around if any weather blows in. That mountain becomes dangerous fast." Being young and overconfident, we pushed on up the mountain regardless of clouds moving in and wind picking up. Nothing was going to stop us from bagging that peak.

Sure enough, as soon as we reached the top, a hail storm kicked in, and my hiking companion twisted his ankle on the now slick terrain. We were woefully unpre-

pared, having little survival knowledge, no first aid kit, and wearing cotton t-shirts and shorts. The whiteout conditions of the sleet and hail mix, and rocky terrain at the peak, made it nearly impossible to locate the trail to get back down. It took us the rest of the day and into the evening to limp off that mountain. By the time we got out, we were dehydrated and in the early stages of hypothermia. We were extremely lucky to have made it out alive!

Not long after that fateful trip, I dived into learning as much as I could about wilderness survival through books and classes. My survival education was life changing. Not only did I gain practical lifesaving skills, but my relationship with nature was completely transformed. Knowing what plants, trees, stones, sticks, and other materials could support my basic needs in a survival situation instilled a profound sense of connection with nature and confidence in my outdoor skills that spilled into every aspect of my life. I knew how to prepare for outings, and everywhere I traveled, I noticed survival resources that had never been part of my awareness before. My survival education experiences gave me the tools to interact with nature more fully, untethered from the fears of the unknown. It was a spring board that propelled me forward into an exciting future.

Little did I know of where that educational trajectory would take me over the years. From studying and practicing survival skills all over the country, to working as a mountain lion biologist, to teaching at wilderness schools, to consulting for survival TV shows, and to the founding of Alderleaf Wilderness College, that trajectory has been an amazing journey that has taken me beyond anything I could have imagined.

My passion now is to pass on these empowering wilderness skills to as many folks as possible but in a much more approachable and efficient format than the piecemeal way I did it. I am so proud of the thousands of students that have come through classes here at Alderleaf. Their survival education opened up deep nature connections and a world of possibility for them as well. I hope this book not only provides you with practical skills but lights a fuse of passion that takes you to amazing places in your life!

IN THIS CHAPTER YOU WILL LEARN TO:

- Deal with fear and panic in a survival situation
- Recognize symptoms of exposure, dehydration, and starvation
- Set survival priorities

About Survival

There are many dimensions to wilderness survival and a myriad of skills. What helps at the beginning of wilderness skills study is to zoom out and look at the big picture. The following survival concepts will put the skills in the other chapters into context, so you can tackle any situation you find yourself in.

What defines a survival situation? A survival situation occurs any time a person's life is threatened by either internal or external factors. This book focuses on wilderness survival situations.

Energy: The body is a carefully controlled balance of energy gain and energy loss. When hiking in the woods, your legs use up energy carrying you around. Later, when you return home, you drink water, eat food, and sleep to restore energy to your body. Being lost in the wilderness becomes a survival situation when opportunities for restoring energy to the body become extremely limited. In addition, the surroundings will often act to drain your energy quickly if preventative action is not taken. Once body temperature or hydration runs too low, you can quickly die.

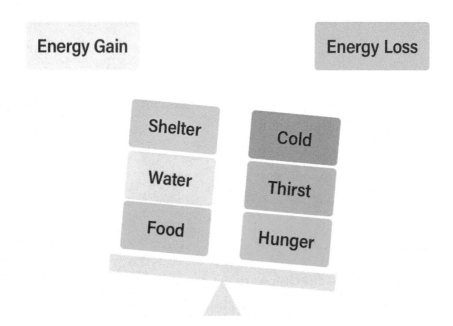

The Psychology of Survival

Arguably, one of the most important aspects of survival is what goes on between your ears. Some call it a positive mental attitude (PMA), an upright mind, high morale, or simply "the will to survive." Regardless of its name, keeping a level head can save lives. This is because fear, anxiety, and panic work against good decision-making. Countless lost persons have perished due to poor decision-making, stemming from a panicked state of mind. This can be combatted with the knowledge, confidence, and self-reliance that come from learning the skills presented in this book. An excellent first step for countering panic is the SPEAR approach.

SPEAR

Using your energy efficiently is important in wilderness survival situations since opportunities to replenish it are likely to be limited. Unfortunately, panic is a common reaction that many people have when they realize that they are lost in the backcountry. A panicked individual often will not make logical nor energy efficient decisions. They may start running or even plunge into cold water at night. A panicked individual has a much higher chance of becoming injured or perishing. To prevent a panic response, memorize the SPEAR acronym.

SPEAR stands for: Stop, Plan, Execute, Assess, and Re-evaluate.

Specifically, this means that when you first suspect you may be in a survival emergency it is important to first stop what you are doing. For example, this might mean admitting you're lost and stopping your hike.

Use this break in activity to think about your situation, the dangers you face, the supplies you have on hand, and the resources available in the surrounding landscape. Then, put together a plan of how to best improve your survival situation. For example, this could be recognizing that it's getting dark and shelter will be needed to avoid hypothermia and survive the night.

Next, engage your mind and body in executing your plan. To continue with the example, this is where you would build the shelter. Engaging in tasks that improve your situation helps calm the mind.

Once you've completed the first task, it's time to assess progress and re-evaluate your survival situation so that you can take on the most important next steps. Continuing with our example, once the shelter is completed, your assessment and re-evaluation may determine that clean water will be your next priority; thus, a fire is now needed to boil water from a stream.

Stop	• Stop what you are doing and look around.
Plan	• Take stock of your supplies, surroundings, and situation. Figure out what you need to do first.
Execute	• Put your plan into action. Engage in improving your situation.
Assess	• Periodically pause to assess your progress and next steps.
Re-evaluate	• Ask yourself if your actions are helping or hindering your survival? Determine what your next needs are.

The SPEAR system works best when you continuously cycle through the steps to keep yourself actively engaged in improving your situation, thereby avoiding panic and reducing fear and anxiety. By maintaining a level head, you massively improve your chances of survival!

Go over these steps in your mind and familiarize yourself with them *before* you end up in a survival situation. Become so familiar with them that they become an automatic response that will override a panicked reaction. SPEAR is not limited to the first minutes or hours of being lost; it can be used repeatedly to confirm that skills are being applied effectively and energy is being used efficiently throughout the survival experience.

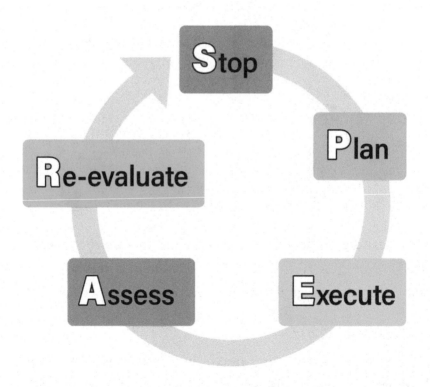

The Three Primary Threats to Survival

Energy is not used up evenly in a survival situation. Some forms of energy drain happen quickly, and some happen slowly. Always remember the Rule of Threes:

The Average Human Can Survive...

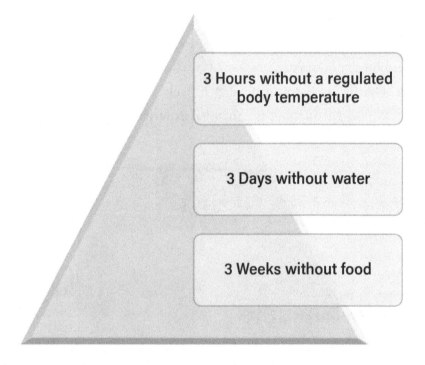

3 Hours without a regulated body temperature

3 Days without water

3 Weeks without food

As you can see, shelter from the elements is a much higher priority than finding water or food right away. The Rule of Threes helps you address threats in a logical and productive order, so you can stay alive!

THREAT #1: Exposure

The average temperature for a healthy human body is 98.6°F. Your body has several mechanisms for maintaining that temperature. For example, sweating cools your skin, burning calories keeps you warm, and having hair helps insulate your head. When these mechanisms are overwhelmed by environmental factors, your body begins to lose energy rapidly. The term *exposure* covers both forms of this threat: *hypothermia* (being too cold) and *hyperthermia* (being too hot).

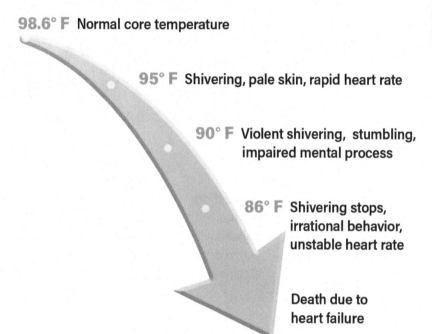

98.6° F Normal core temperature

95° F Shivering, pale skin, rapid heart rate

90° F Violent shivering, stumbling, impaired mental process

86° F Shivering stops, irrational behavior, unstable heart rate

Death due to heart failure

Hypothermia:

This condition occurs when the body's core temperature drops down below 95°F. Early symptoms include involuntary shivering, pale skin, and increased heart rate. In a survival situation, you should take preventative action before early symptoms start to appear. Moderate symptoms include violent shivering, loss of coordination, and mental confusion as your core temperature continues to drop. Many people cannot rewarm themselves at this stage if they are alone. Their impaired mental state and lack of dexterity tend to prevent them from building a fire or a shelter. Severe symptoms include significant mental impairment and irrational behavior, a cessation of shivering, and a high, unstable heart rate. Unconsciousness and death soon follow. **Hypothermia is the most common cause of death in documented wilderness survival scenarios.**

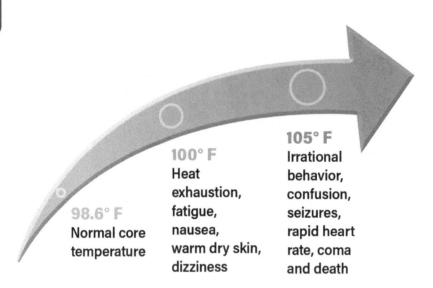

98.6° F
Normal core
temperature

100° F
Heat
exhaustion,
fatigue,
nausea,
warm dry skin,
dizziness

105° F
Irrational
behavior,
confusion,
seizures,
rapid heart
rate, coma
and death

Hyperthermia:

This condition occurs when your core temperature rises above 100°F, roughly. This can generally occur in excessively hot and humid environments, especially when combined with exercise and dehydration. Mild symptoms (also known as heat exhaustion) include hot dry skin, nausea, vomiting, fatigue, and headaches. **Once again, in a survival situation, you should take preventative action before early symptoms start to appear.** Severe symptoms include confusion, hostility, irrational behavior, seizures, rapid heart rate, coma, and death. Core temperatures above 105°F can be lethal.

THREAT #2: Dehydration

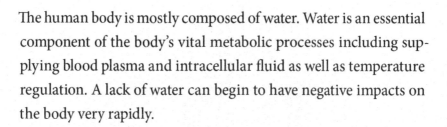

Healthy Hydration
Urination clear and frequent

Mild Dehydration
Decreased urine output and quality,
dry mouth, irritability, thirst

Severe Dehydration
Sleepiness, no urine, dry skin,
loss of vision, seizures
and death

The human body is mostly composed of water. Water is an essential component of the body's vital metabolic processes including supplying blood plasma and intracellular fluid as well as temperature regulation. A lack of water can begin to have negative impacts on the body very rapidly.

Mild symptoms include thirst, headache, dizziness, decreased urine volume, dark urine, dry mouth, and irritability. Many people walk around mildly dehydrated in their everyday lives.

Severe dehydration is accompanied by lethargy or extreme sleepiness, lack of urination, dry shrunken skin, tingling in the limbs, loss of vision, and can cause seizures and death. A healthy, hydrated human being should be urinating every three to five hours and should have light colored or clear urine. The amount of water required to achieve this varies according to the level of physical activity performed and the local environmental conditions.

THREAT #3: Starvation

Often in a wilderness survival situation, starvation is the least of many worries. Not only because it takes so long to seriously threaten your health, but also because there are many edible plants and animals in nearly all locations and habitats. However, hunger can have a serious negative impact on morale during a wilderness survival scenario.

Symptoms of starvation include rapid weight loss of both muscle and fat tissue, fatigue, irritability, and impulsivity. The sensation of hunger fades as the stomach atrophies during the early stages of starvation.

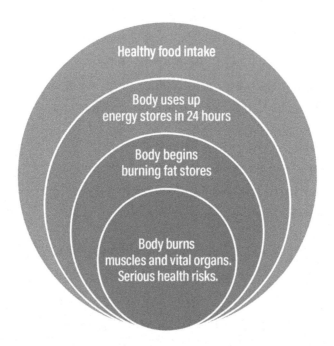

Severe starvation is accompanied by vitamin deficiencies (which can cause a host of other health problems), atrophied muscles, sore joints, permanent organ damage, and extreme fatigue or stupor. Eventually, the victim is so weak that they cannot or will not react to stimuli. Dehydration often accompanies late-stage starvation. Death follows soon after.

Starvation is a fairly uncommon cause of death in documented wilderness survival situations. Hypothermia and dehydration are far more common.

Survival Priorities

Using the Rule of Threes, you can empower yourself to confront and prevent the three threats to life in a wilderness survival scenario. Hypothermia is the quickest way to lose energy to the environment, so a warm, dry shelter is the top priority. Dehydration can affect the body within a day and can kill you in three days, so water is the next priority. Fire can be used to further heat a shelter or to purify water, among other things, so it is the third priority in many situations. Starvation takes a long time to damage the body, so food is the last priority.

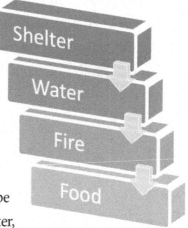

A large group shelter

Boiling water with hot rocks

Survival Priority #1: Shelter

A shelter should be built according to your needs and the environment. If you are in a temperate or cold area, its chief function is to keep you warm and dry. If you are in a tropical or desert environment, its chief function is to provide protection from the sun.

Survival Priority #2: Water

The most common way to obtain water is from surface sources (lakes, streams, and rivers). Surface water should be purified to avoid getting sick from water-borne pathogens, which can seriously reduce the chances of survival. Water can also be obtained from springs, rain catchment, dew, and plant sources.

Fire performs many functions

Nettles are a valuable edible plant

Survival Priority #3: Fire

Fire can do many things for you in a survival scenario. It can provide heat for your shelter, allow you to dry wet clothes, purify water through boiling, cook your food, and signal rescuers. Fire is also an important tool for combating mental discomfort and boosting poor morale in the wilderness.

Fire can move around on the priority list according to your needs. For example, if you need to purify drinking water without modern equipment, then fire may need to come before water on your priorities list so that you can boil the water.

Survival Priority #4: Food

Food is the lowest priority in a survival situation. It generally takes a long time to starve to death. Only after all of your other priorities are met should food-gathering become a focus. In a wilderness survival situation, the easiest sources of food are often wild edible plants. Proteins and fat can be harder to come by. Gathering insects and catching small game (like snakes and frogs) is often the least difficult option for protein. Setting traps and hunting large game are often more complex and energy intensive.

KNOWLEDGE

Know Your Environment

All survival skills require a certain amount of background education in order to be used to their full potential. Having a strong grasp of local plant and animal knowledge will make life a lot easier in the backcountry. Before heading out into the wilderness, it is a good idea to familiarize yourself with some of the local plants, animals, and hazards you may encounter. It could literally save your life.

Know How to Navigate

Anyone who routinely enters the backcountry should have a strong grasp of basic map and compass use. Always study a map of the area you will be entering and carry one with you if possible.

Know How to Satisfy Your Survival Priorities

Study the skills presented in the following chapters, extensively, before going out and entering any potentially dangerous situations. Real wilderness survival situations are not glamorous or fun, and they can be fatal.

CHAPTER SUMMARY

- Use a SPEAR (Stop, Plan, Execute, Assess, and Re-evaluate) to avoid panicking.

- The Rule of Threes determines survival priorities (a person can survive roughly three hours without a regulated body temperature, three days without water, and three weeks without food).

- The primary survival threats include are exposure (hypothermia/hyperthermia), dehydration, and starvation.

- Survival priorities (in order of importance) are shelter, water, fire, and food.

CHAPTER 2

Survival Shelter

M any survival situations require a shelter to be built as the first task. A shelter offers protection from the elements and the dangers of hypothermia—the primary threat to survival—while providing a place to get a good night's rest. It also creates a central hub to your camp, helping you stay in place while waiting for search and rescue teams to find you.

A few years into my wilderness survival studies, a passionate group of fellow survival enthusiasts decided to plan an extended trip to practice food-gathering survival skills. We had already spent many weekends together building and staying in natural shelters, making fires, and purifying water to address the primary needs of short-term survival emergencies. The group felt ready to focus on the longer-term survival challenge of procuring calorie-rich wild foods.

It was in the middle of a warm summer when we headed up into the mountains to spend a week in the backcountry. Upon arriving at a suitable meadow near a giant cattail swamp, we began setting up camp. To my surprise, the group decided a *shelter was not needed due to the warm weather, and they were eager to start foraging, fishing, and trapping. The decision was to simply sleep next to the fire out under the stars.*

Half the group, including myself, barely slept a wink that first night, due to cold nighttime temperatures and winds. In addition, there wasn't enough space for eight people to sleep close enough to the fire to benefit from its warmth. Surprisingly, the group could not be convinced to build a shelter the next day, due to overwhelming desires to spend the day fishing, building survival traps and snares, and digging cattail roots and other edible plants. Half of our group pulled together to build a stacked debris wall (a waist-high wall made out of sticks and leaves), in a circle around the fire pit area. At least the wall would buffer some of the winds and reflect some of the heat from the fire.

Unfortunately, the second night, with its lower temperatures and stronger winds, was even worse than the first. The lack of a full shelter still left us exposed. By day three, many of us were so exhausted from two nights of exposure and no sleep that we became ill! Our hopes for a productive practice survival trip had become a suffer-fest, and we no longer had the energy and health to focus on harvesting wild foods.

If we had simply started the trip with building a shelter, we would have been able to stay warm, sleep well, and avoid getting sick. Most importantly, we would have had the energy needed to tackle all the planned wild-food-gathering activities. The lesson of this trip is that, no matter how warm it is during the day and no matter how practiced you are in the basics, it's important, first and foremost, to take the time to appropriately address your primary survival need of shelter.

IN THIS CHAPTER YOU WILL LEARN ABOUT:

- The importance of shelter and body heat retention

- The ways your body loses heat and how it informs shelter design

- Debris hut shelter construction with step-by-step instructions

- Shelter effectiveness with tips and tricks for improvement

Forms of Heat Loss

With hypothermia being the most important concern in almost any survival scenario, creating a shelter that reduces heat loss in all its forms is key. The five primary forms of heat loss are radiation, conduction, convection, respiration, and evaporation. Here's how they apply to survival shelters.

1. **Radiation.** Heat loss through radiation happens because our bodies are typically warmer than the surrounding environment. Heat simply rises off of us. A good shelter can reduce this form of heat loss by insulating the areas all around our bodies, especially above them. This can be achieved by piling lots of dry leaves (or other debris such as ferns, mosses, grasses, pine needles, etc.) all around us inside the shelter and using lots of debris as part of the ceiling/roof.

2. Conduction. Conductive heat loss is when heat transfers from one solid to another solid. In survival, this means that when you sit or lay on the ground, heat is transferring out of your body and into the colder ground. To reduce this form of heat loss, an insulating layer must be created, a mattress so-to-speak, out of natural materials to create a thermal break from the ground. This is accomplished by piling up debris into a mattress shape to sit and lie on.

3. Convection. Convection is when heat is lost or gained by air flow. In survival, this often equates to your body losing heat rapidly when exposed to wind. A good shelter offers protection from the wind. This can be accomplished in several ways, such as building in a location naturally protected from the wind; creating a thick layer of natural debris that the wind cannot penetrate; or adding a layer of wind resistant natural materials to your shelter's exterior, such as slabs of bark or a layer of mud.

4. Respiration. We all lose heat due to respiration because the air we breathe *in* is typically cooler than our body temperature, and the air we breathe *out* has been warmed in our lungs. By having a mostly sealed interior space, a survival shelter can reduce this form of heat loss and take advantage of respiration as a heat source. For snow shelters this means employing only small vents for fresh air. For debris shelters this means making sure the doorway is sealed most of the way. When the amount of air coming in and out of a shelter is reduced, your own body heat and respiration can help warm the inside of the shelter, reducing heat loss, while still allowing enough fresh air to flow to the inside.

5. Evaporation. Body heat is lost incredibly fast when your skin gets wet. For survival situations, this means avoiding sweating or having skin directly contacting wet clothes. While building survival shelters, it is important to shed layers if you get warm and to work at a pace that is below the threshold of sweating. This will assure dry clothing. In addition, a good survival shelter offers protection from

precipitation. Again, this can be accomplished in several ways: by building in a location naturally protected from the weather; creating a thick layer of debris on the shelter roof that rain and snow cannot penetrate; or by adding a layer of water-resistant materials to the exterior such as slabs of bark from a dead tree arranged in a shingling pattern.

Shelter Considerations

In planning out a survival shelter, there are several aspects that must be taken into consideration first:

Location

As in real estate, location is everything. It absolutely must be clear of hazards such as falling branches, yellow jacket ground nests, or low spots where rainwater might pool during a storm. It should also be surrounded by an abundance of the materials you plan to use to build the shelter, such as leaves, sticks, or moss. In other words, don't carry branches from a mile away to build a shelter.

Insulation

It is important to plan out how you will insulate yourself from the ground, the wind, and from precipitation. Decide which natural materials will be used for the walls, roof, floor, bedding, and doorway. Be sure the location can supply necessary quantities of these materials.

Heat Source

Determine whether the shelter will be warmed by body heat or by the heat of a fire. Shelters heated by body heat are typically compact and full of debris, like a giant mummy style sleeping bag. In contrast, fire-heated shelters are either open to a fire on one side (a lean-to) or are relatively open on the inside, with a higher ceiling and smoke hole (such as a debris tipi). Other considerations for fire-heated shelters include acquiring enough firewood to last each night and formulating a plan of how the fire will get tended to keep it going all night (and to ensure that the shelter doesn't catch fire!).

Personal or Group Shelter

Determine whether the shelter will be for one person or will need to be large enough for a group. If you are with several others, we've found the most efficient shelter size to be a three- to six-person group shelter . These shelters can be built faster than multiple individual shelters or huge group shelters.

Types of Shelters

There are many options for survival shelters. The following is an overview of a few that are favorites at Alderleaf:

Natural Shelters

Natural shelters are places that are already functioning as a good shelter, such as caves or very large hollowed out stumps. If available, they are an excellent choice in a survival situation because they can be used quickly with few modifications. For example, a hollow stump may already be dry and protected from the wind

Cedar stump natural shelter

and rain. Adding some insulating debris may be all that is needed. For another example, a cave may be ready to go by just building a mattress, closing in the open side, and building a fire for heat.

Lean-To Shelters

This simple shelter is a roof/wall structure made from sticks and debris (leaves, moss, ferns, evergreen boughs, and other materials) with a debris mattress inside and a fire in front. A lean-to is often

A debris covered lean-to

a one- or two-person shelter. The slope of the roof should be approximately 45 degrees, which is steep enough to shed water, yet not so steep that debris slides off.

Debris Tipis

Like the name implies, this survival shelter is a tipi made of sticks and debris. It is also a fire-heated shelter, and it typically hosts a group of three to six people. It is our favorite shelter for group survival trips because it provides so

Finishing construction of a debris tipi

much insulation and protection from the elements. Again, the roof slope should be at about a 45-degree angle.

Snow Shelters

Snow is an excellent insulating material. Snow shelters come in many forms, such as the quinzee (pictured), snow cave, and snow trench. Regardless of form, snow shelters require a door that is lower than the sleeping

A completed quinzee

area. Because warm air rises and cold air sinks, the low door is necessary to trap warm air inside and to allow cold air to drain out. It is important to insulate the floor of the shelter from the snow by building a mattress of evergreen boughs or other materials.

Debris Huts

The debris hut is one of the most practical, versatile survival shelters. It is effective in warm, cool, and cold climates and can be built in almost any environment. The debris shelter typically fits one or two people and is warmed by body heat.

Four stages of debris hut construction

How to Build a Debris Hut Survival Shelter

Because of its widespread usefulness, the debris hut is the most important shelter to learn to build. This shelter is meant to perform like a large sleeping bag, so it is essential to keep the interior just big enough to fit your body. The debris hut is designed to use your own body heat for warmth. Its layers of debris trap air and insulate you from the elements.

Step 1: Location

The first consideration for building any survival shelter is location. To recap, the ideal spot should have most of the following characteristics:

- very near or at a spot with an abundance of the necessary materials including lots of debris (such as dead leaves, moss, ferns, etc.), plenty of sticks of different sizes, and some potential ridge poles (described later);

- away from hazards like large cottonwood, alder, or beech trees that are known to drop large limbs (called widowmakers);

- away from the nests of ants or wasps;

- away from creek sides and riversides or similar locations where water can rise swiftly;

- away from low points in the landscape that may pool up with water during rainstorms.

Once an ideal spot is found (with the characteristics listed above and plenty of the raw materials you need), start looking for a solid ridgepole.

Step 2: The Ridgepole

Find a very strong, straight tree limb to use as a ridge pole. It can be made from a downed log or branch, standing dead tree, or even a live tree that is cut down. This is the supporting *spine* along which the rest of the shelter will be built. It should be about eight feet long. It is important that the ridge pole be strong enough to support your entire body weight without breaking. Test it by carefully standing on the ridgepole when it is leaning at an angle. Or to be safer, test the strength of the ridgepole by suspending your full body weight on it from underneath.

Testing the ridgepole strength with body weight   *A safer approach to testing the ridgepole strength*

After testing the strength of the ridge pole, it is time to place it on a nearby stump, a fork in a tree, or other similarly supportive structure. The high end of the ridge pole should be about waist height with the other end slanting down to the ground. Adjust the length of the ridge-pole and the placement of the bottom end of the ridgepole until it has the right span to fit your body underneath without much extra space.

Once it has been placed at an appropriate angle, it is a good idea to crawl underneath the ridge pole to gauge the dimensions of the hut. The ridgepole should touch the ground just past your feet with enough clearance that the tops of your shoes don't poke above the ridgepole. If needed, prop up the bottom end with a stone or piece of wood to create enough space for your feet. Mark the ground approximately six inches out from both sides of your body by placing sticks on the ground (see the photo). This is where the ribbing sticks, referenced in an upcoming step, will touch the ground. This will help you visualize the hut's inner footprint more clearly.

Yes, it is true that debris huts are supposed to be snug; however, they should not be so cramped that you can't straighten your legs or turn over.

Gauging the dimensions of the debris hut

Once the ridgepole is secured and at the proper angle, move on to the next steps.

Step 3: Debris Mattress

Pile up at least eight to twelve inches of debris (such as dead leaves, mosses, ferns, soft evergreen branches) within the footprint of the shelter (the floor). This step is essential for the hut to be effective at keeping you warm. This mattress of debris provides insulation from the ground, which can be a major source of heat loss. Dry, fluffy material is preferable.

Debris mattress

Step 4: Ribbing

It is now time to add ribbing sticks to the ridgepole spine. It is important that these ribs are the appropriate lengths for the shelter. They should span the space between the ground and the ridgepole without extending past the ridgepole. Gather several large armfuls of sticks of various lengths that are about two finger widths thick at a minimum. They must be strong enough to support the weight of the debris that will be placed over them. Place them down the spine.

It is best to have the ribs as close as possible to each other. This will help prevent debris from falling through later on in the construction process. Take a look at the next photo.

Debris hut ribbing in place

Be sure that the ribs rest on the ridgepole at about a 45-degree angle; any steeper, and the debris will likely fall off. At a shallower angle, water will likely find its way through the debris. Also, be sure that the ends of the ribs don't stick up very far past the ridgepole; if they do, this can channel water into the shelter during heavy rain. It is best to cut or break off these ends so they only stick a few inches past the ridgepole at most. Continue placing the ribs and remember to leave a space for a door.

Step 5: The Doorway

A debris hut doorway

A doorway is created at the taller end of your shelter, near where your head will rest when inside. To prevent drafts from entering the shelter, take note of the dominant wind direction in the area and try to orient the doorway on the opposite side from the prevailing winds.

It's very important to keep the doorway small. It should be just big enough for you to fit your shoulders through and no larger. This will reduce heat loss and make it easier to plug the door when you crawl in for the night. Make the doorway as low and small as possible without restricting your ability to climb into and out of the shelter.

A doorway can be created by simply leaving a small gap where there are no ribs.

Step 6: Latticework

This step requires more armloads of sticks. This time, however, they should be long, thin, feathery branches. Place these latticework sticks on top of the ribbing in different directions (they should rest on top of the ribbing, not woven into it). As you construct the latticework, the shelter will start to look like it's covered with a web of long thin sticks. This latticework of sticks is what will hold the debris in place.

In the next photo, a latticework of downed hemlock boughs is laid in place. It is best to place several overlapping layers of latticework on the shelter to minimize debris falling through. Make sure to cover all of the ribbing areas, including on both sides of and above the door.

Placing the lattice work on the ribbing

Step 7: Debris—The Key to a Warm Shelter

Piling up a tremendous amount of debris on top of the latticework is a vital step in successful shelter construction and requires the most amount of time and effort. Debris is basically any kind of fluffy material available, including leaf litter, small conifer boughs, ferns, mosses, pine needles, or even grasses. Gather many arm loads of debris for this step. Once you have covered the entire shelter with a thick layer of debris, poke your head inside to inspect where light may be coming in. Add material to those spots. Continue checking

Gauging the depth of debris

and adding more material until no more light filters through. The more debris that is added, the warmer the shelter will be.

At what point do you know you have enough debris? Three feet of debris depth on all sides of the shelter is a measure to aim for. Three feet is about fingertip to armpit. A good way to test the debris depth is to gently work your fingers into the material and move them down and in until you feel the ribs. When you do so, is the debris all the way out to your armpit? If not, then keep adding more!

Remember, the more debris that is in place, the better insulated you will be inside the shelter. Collecting large amounts each time you grab debris is much more energy efficient than collecting many smaller amounts. It might even be worth using a large garbage bag, jacket, or tarp to help gather large amounts of debris. Improvise with what you have. If nothing else, just grab large armloads.

Next, pack the inside of the shelter with dry debris, on top of the debris mattress, all the way to the ceiling. This inner debris needs to contact your body on all sides (except your face) so that you are insulated and kept warm. Any large dead airspaces inside the shelter will become cold spots if they are not filled with debris. You want to be able to burrow your way, feet first, into the structure and to have plenty of insulating debris all around you.

Step 8: Plugging the Doorway

Once you have a sufficient amount of debris insulating the shelter, start thinking about how to plug the doorway. It is vital to have some means of plugging up the doorway once you have crawled inside the hut. One way is to fill a bag or extra jacket with debris. If the hole is small enough, a backpack can be used. Or if those options are not available, simply make a really large pile of debris and pull it into the doorway as you crawl inside. The next photos show a door plug made of woven ferns and branches.

Always enter a debris hut shelter feet first, being careful not to disturb the debris walls. Entering feet first allows the use of your arms to seal up the doorway as you crawl in.

Additional Considerations

In wet conditions, it can be helpful to kindle a small fire outside the shelter, during the construction process, where you can dry debris before putting it inside the shelter. Pile the debris around the fire, turning it over periodically so that the heat from the fire dries out the material, then stuff it inside the shelter. This will increase your comfort and help you get a better night's sleep.

Now that your debris hut shelter is completed, test it out! Try sleeping in it a few nights and make adjustments to the interior and exterior until you feel it is in optimal shape. There are many subtle skills that can be learned only through this kind of practice. Try sleeping in the shelter during a variety of weather conditions including rain and even snow. Also, try out different kinds of insulating materials for both the inside and outside of the hut.

Always be safe when practicing survival skills. Take a sleeping bag or wool blanket along in case you get too cold during the night. If you start to shiver or feel too uncomfortable, get out of the shelter and rewarm yourself with some jumping jacks or jogging in place. Then climb back into the shelter with your backup sleeping bag or blanket. Also, tell people that you are sleeping in a debris shelter so they know where you are and when you will be back in the morning.

Troubleshooting Tips

Is the shelter leaking when it rains?

This can be caused by several factors. First, there may not be enough insulation on the shelter. Add more debris and observe the changes. If this is not solving the problem, consider looking more closely at the *angle* at which the ribs were placed. Are they at about a 45-degree angle? If not, it might be worth your time to take all the debris off of the shelter carefully and adjust the rib angles. This may also require collecting more ribs, since you may find that some of them are too short or too long.

Another possible source of dripping problems can be the *length* of the shelter ribs. How long are your ribs, and how far do they stick out beyond the ridge pole? If they do stick out considerably beyond the edge of the ridge pole, they must be shortened. Remember, no more than a few inches beyond the ridge pole; otherwise, the ribs become channels for water to run down and drip into the interior.

Is your shelter cold?

An obvious cause of a cold interior would be insufficient debris on the outside of your shelter. If you find that the quantity of debris on the outside is adequate (at least three feet thick), consider looking at other possibilities. Perhaps the shelter is too large on the inside, and therefore, the warm air is not kept close enough to your body. This can be fixed by rebuilding the shelter at a smaller scale or by stuffing extra debris *inside* your shelter. In addition, heat loss via conduction can be minimized by ensuring that your body is well insulated from the cold ground with a thick debris mattress. If you skimp on debris inside, even three feet of debris on the outside of the shelter will likely not keep you warm.

If you are lying on wet debris, you will likely be colder. For the interior of the shelter, be sure to choose the driest and fluffiest materials you can find. If that is not possible, consider drying out some or all of it by a fire.

In Conclusion

As with all survival skills, shelter building requires practice in the field to build your confidence and proficiency. Invite your friends and enjoy practicing shelter building together! Many hands make light work, differing viewpoints can produce useful observations, and it's lots of fun.

CHAPTER SUMMARY

- Shelter is often the number one survival priority due to the need to prevent hypothermia.

- All five forms of heat loss should be considered when planning a survival shelter: radiation, conduction, convection, respiration, and evaporation.

- Additional shelter considerations include avoiding hazards, building near materials, selecting a heat source (body heat or fire heat), and whether to build an individual or group shelter.

- Popular shelter types include naturally occurring shelters, lean-to structures, debris tipis, snow shelters, and the debris hut.

- The debris hut is one of the most versatile shelters and can be created in nearly any environment. The debris hut consists of a ridgepole, ribbing sticks, fine latticework sticks, lots of debris inside and outside the hut, and a doorway plug.

CHAPTER 3

Survival Water Purification

Almost all water in the wilderness is contaminated with microorganisms. I have several survival friends who believed they could get away with drinking straight from streams and springs without purification only to contract debilitating Giardia and suffer from subsequent chronic health problems. Sure, some may get away with drinking nonfiltered water a few times; however, this practice is a form of Russian roulette that will eventually catch up with them. So, it is imperative to treat wild water, which is why I boil water when on primitive survival outings and bring water filtration systems when on regular camping trips.

Unfortunately, I learned the importance of water purification in a more personal way. In the spring of 2005, while on a camping trip up the Skykomish River, I used a water bottle that featured a built-in water filter. I was able to scoop up river water with the bottle and squeeze it through the filter any time I needed a drink. However, about midway *through the trip, I noticed a strange gurgling sound when drinking from the bottle. After having finished most of the water, I finally investigated the odd sound. Upon taking apart the bottle, I discovered a broken rubber seal that allowed water to bypass the filter entirely. I had just drunk nearly an entire bottle of untreated river water!*

Luckily, soon after discovering the failure of the filter, I had the foresight to hike out while I was still capable of doing so under my own power. Sure enough, by the next day, I was quite sick with nausea, vomiting, diarrhea, and fever. This acute level of sickness can turn a regular survival challenge into a deadly situation. Thankfully, I was able to make it home, meet with a doctor, and procure the medicines necessary to deal with the pathogens. I recovered safely at home over the following days.

Water purification is of the utmost importance in any wilderness activity. Don't learn the hard way, make it a top priority from the start.

IN THIS CHAPTER YOU WILL LEARN ABOUT:

- The importance of water
- The dangers of dehydration
- Types of water contamination
- Methods of water purification
- The burned-bowl rock-boiling method of water purification, with step-by-step instructions

Water Is a High Priority

Because a person can only live for three days (on average) without water, it is number two on our list of survival priorities. Many people who get lost suffer from dehydration and water borne pathogens that come from untreated water. Even one day without water will greatly reduce mental performance and can lead to impaired judgment.

The human body needs three to four liters of water a day to be fully hydrated. It is always a good idea to start any hiking or camping trip fully hydrated. However, be aware that overhydrating by drinking too much water too fast can be damaging to the body. It is much better to drink smaller amounts of water more often, since overhydrating causes an imbalance with natural sodium and electrolytes. Electrolytes may be replaced with foods high in simple sugars. But if water is not available for extended periods, do not eat; the body uses a lot of water to process food and eating can lead to a more serious case of dehydration.

Types of Water Contamination

- Biological (such as Giardia, Cryptosporidium, and E. coli)
- Chemical
- Mineral

Giardia and Cryptosporidium are both fairly common parasites that can cause long-term intestinal discomfort and uncontrollable diarrhea if left untreated. Symptoms appear anywhere from one to fourteen days after ingesting the contaminated water. Giardia and E. coli are water borne pathogens that are passed via fecal matter and may even be present in fast moving or clear water. E. coli is a bacterium found in the intestinal tract of most animals (including humans). It is an essential part of the digestive process in the lower digestive tract (the large intestine and colon). If E. coli is introduced into the upper digestive tract (the stomach) it can cause severe diarrhea. E. coli symptoms appear within one to two days and can be life threatening. Luckily, E. coli cannot live for long periods of time outside of a host organism.

If it is not known what may be upstream from a water source, it is best not to take the risk of consuming the water. Mineral and heavy metal contaminants can be found downstream from agricultural and industrial operations. These contaminants tend to pose more long-term risks (e.g., cancer) when compared to the short-term risks posed by biological contaminants. However, high mineral content in water can also cause severe diarrhea and vomiting, both of which speed up dehydration.

Water Sources

In survival situations, the following are good sources of wild water:

Natural springs

These are spots where groundwater comes to the surface. This water can be safe to drink untreated if it has not had a chance to become contaminated. Springs in high elevations that do not have vegetation growing around them and are not downslope from ponds are the least risky. Most springs (especially those with vegetation growing around them) should be considered contaminated with microorganisms. Water from them should be treated.

Headwaters

These are the beginnings of streams, the uppermost parts of water systems farthest from main rivers. The chances of seasonal headwater streams being contaminated may be lower than larger creeks and rivers; however, treating this water will ensure your safety.

Dew

Early morning dew can be collected from nonpoisonous plant leaves using a bandana, t-shirt, or sponge. The dew is then squeezed from the collector into a container or directly into your mouth to drink. A surprisingly large volume of water can be attained by collecting dew early in the morning. This water is typically clean enough to drink untreated because it has been evaporated and then condensed much like a home distillation process.

Snow

Rather than eating snow directly, it should be melted over a campfire or stove before consumption. Eating snow directly causes the body to work really hard to heat and melt the snow, which can lead to further dehydration.

Sip Well

A good source of water can often be found by digging a hole in moist areas such as near seeps or run offs. This hole, called a sip well, should fill with ground water. Groundwater near the surface has the chance of being contaminated, so it is best to purify water from a sip well.

Rainwater

In many survival situations, a clean tarp, jacket, or vessel can be used to collect rainwater. Rainwater is typically safe to drink as long as it is collected in a clean container and is not allowed to sit out for hours since bacteria grows in still water. If there's any question as to how clean the container is or for how long the water has been sitting, then it is best to purify it as a precaution.

Water Purification

Today, there are many options for purifying water.

Chemical treatments, including the use of iodine; different types of filtering devices from pumps to filtering straws; and hybrid systems that combine filters with chemical treatment. Small micron filters are typically sufficient in wilderness areas because they remove all pathogens except the smallest viruses, and viruses tend to be rare in wilderness areas. The added benefit of chemical components like iodine is that they will rid the water of all viruses too. These methods are very effective if accessible in a survival situation.

Purifying water via UV light is becoming a popular option. It requires very clear water to be effective and is battery powered. We don't recommend UV light systems because water found in the wilderness is often not perfectly clear and batteries can run out or go bad.

Herbal treatment is another possible way to purify water; however, there is conflicting research and debate on whether or not herbal treatments are effective. People have used antimicrobial herbs like Oregon grape root and grapefruit seed extract to reduce pathogens in water. Grapefruit seed extract is sold in some stores. However, there are lab tests indicating that the reported antimicrobial actions are due to chemical solvents used in the extraction process instead of the actual grapefruit seed oils. We would not recommend herbal water purification as a primary method. Herbal purification techniques should only be used as a last resort, when no other alternative is available, since they only reduce the risk of illness from contaminated water rather than being completely effective.

The most widely approved and used method for safely purifying water is boiling. Most waterborne organisms are destroyed at hot temperatures a bit below the boiling point, but for safety reasons, water should always be brought to a full rolling boil. If a metal water bottle or a cooking pot is available, purification via boiling can be achieved over a fire or stove.

Burned-Bowl Water Purification

Burned-bowl water purification is the most reliable method for treating water when you have no modern equipment on hand. You will need:

- a campfire;

- two seasoned softwood logs or rounds for burning in cavities. (Examples of softwoods include pines, cottonwoods, and alders; however, avoid any toxic tree species such as western yew);

- several golf-ball-sized rocks (use nonporous stones; porous stones or stones submerged in water can crack apart or even explode when heated due to expanding interior moisture);

- tongs made from a live branch about two feet long and one inch in diameter that has been bent in half to form the tongs. The inside edges of the tips can be carved flat to help them better grip stones;

- (optional) a primitive straw. This can be made from a branch with a hollow core, such as horsetail or bamboo. Be sure to avoid making a straw from a poisonous plant such as poison hemlock.

Step-by-step instructions:

1. Get a medium or large-sized fire going to provide plenty of hot coals for burning the bowls and heating the rocks.

2. Find two seasoned softwood logs that have a diameter of at least eight inches. This size will be wide enough for burning a bowl-shaped depression that would have a volume of about half a gallon (so that it can hold a quart of water plus the hot rocks without spilling). You can use a fallen dead tree, a piece of driftwood, or use a cut log round.

3. Begin burning out the bowl by taking coals from the fire and placing them on the log where the bowl will be. You can burn into the log from the side or the end of the log (as pictured). Either way is fine. It's a good idea to use a stick or piece of bark to stabilize the pile of coals on the log when first getting started. Once the coals are in place, blow gently toward the bottom of the pile. The coals should be glowing, but keep them from flaming by blowing out any flames. If flames are not kept to a minimum, the extra heat can crack the wood, which can lead to a leaky vessel. With a primitive straw, you can direct the air flow to heat up a very spe-

Blowing on coals in the vessel

Using a straw to increase heat

cific area. The straw also helps to keep your face farther away from the heat.

4. Once you have burned the surface for about ten to fifteen minutes, use the sharp edge of a rock or stick to scrape away the charcoal (carbonized wood). Repeat this burning and scraping process until the bowl cavity is formed to a volume of about a half gallon. It can take at least an hour to make a burn bowl and it's best to take your time rather than rush. You want to control what part of the log burns so that you leave about an inch or more of thickness between the inside of the bowl and the outside of the log. If the wall of the vessel becomes too thin, cracking can occur, allowing water to leak out.

5. Repeat step 3 for the second log (or you can burn in both logs at the same time).

6. Place about six golf-ball-sized rocks in the fire. This number of rocks should be enough to boil about a quart of water.

7. Once the bowls have been burned deep enough to have a volume of about a half gallon and the rocks are red-hot (heating rocks can take about an hour), put a quart of unpurified water from a creek or other source into both bowls. This will leave enough space in the vessel for the water to rise without spilling when the hot rocks are added.

8. Then, one at a time, use the tongs to pull a red-hot rock out of the fire, quickly dip the rock into the first bowl of water to remove any ash stuck to the stone (this first bowl is your cleaning water), then put the cleaned hot rock into the second bowl (which contains the water being purified). To clarify, this first bowl of water will not be boiled nor used for drinking, it is just for cleaning off ash. Additionally, to get even more ash off of the hot rocks, you can quickly wipe them with a leafy branch prior to dunking. It is important to remove most of the ash from each hot stone prior to putting it into the water to be boiled and drunk (a little bit of

ash is fine). Too much ash and water can mix to create lye, which can cause chemical burns if consumed!

9. Once most of the ash is cleaned off the hot stone, drop it into the bowl containing the water you will boil and drink. Continue adding stones, one at a time, until the water boils.

Cleaning bowl left, boiling bowl right with Douglas fir needles added for flavor and nutritional value

Water boiling from hot rocks

The above left photo shows two separate burn bowls, one for cleaning the ash off the rocks and the other for boiling the drinking water. In the above right photo, it is clear that the water has reached a full rolling boil.

10. Once the water has boiled, remove the hot stones to stop the water from continuing to evaporate. Allow the water to cool down before drinking. Once the water has cooled down some, a small handful of green needles from a pine, fir, or spruce tree can be added to impart a pleasant flavor (as well as adding vitamin C). Do not add needles while the water is still boiling because this can extract harmful essential oils. Alternatively, mint leaves or other aromatic edible plants can be used to flavor the water. The

water can be consumed immediately (as soon as it is cool enough to drink) or saved for later in a water bottle.

It may seem like a significant project, however there is nothing like quenching your thirst with water you know firsthand is safe.

CHAPTER SUMMARY

- Dehydration is the second most dangerous threat to survival.

- Adequate clean drinking water is survival priority #2.

- Most water found in the wilderness is contaminated by microorganisms.

- Wild water needs to be purified by either filtration, chemical treatment, or boiling.

- Boiling water with hot rocks in burned bowls is the most effective primitive technique for wild water purification if modern means are not available.

CHAPTER 4

Survival Fire Making

D uring my college years in the late 1990s, I palled around with a circle of friends who, for better or worse, were obsessed with pushing the limits of primitive survival training. We committed to challenges such as only starting fires with friction (no lighters or matches) and not wearing raincoats. A few even went so far as to not use metal knives (only stone knives), go without shoes in the outdoors (only barefoot), and to wear only t-shirts and shorts even on the coldest days of winter.

All of this was with good intentions and to serve our goals of getting better at primitive survival skills, acclimating our bodies to the outdoors, and solving survival challenges with only resources found in the forest, without modern equipment. I say "for better or worse" because a lot of the challenges we set for ourselves were dangerous and not the kind of training I would recommend to anyone now that I look back with more years of experience. However, many of these experiences did serve to highlight the critical value of core survival skills.

On one such outing with my survival friends, we had headed out into the foothills of western Washington early on a winter day. Our goal was to reach a remote waterfall to see if it might harbor freshwater mussels (a prized survival food) in the plunge pool formed at the base of the waterfall. We also planned to look for fresh mountain lion tracks along the way.

As was customary for us, we improvised and took different routes on the way there and back to challenge our navigation skills and to see new territory. And as usual, we did not dress for the weather nor bring any gear with us. This was an approach we all felt comfortable doing since each of us had already been practicing survival skills for several years (in hindsight, we still should have brought back-up gear!).

Sure enough, as we were returning from the waterfall, we got temporarily turned around and hit some dead-end trails that slowed our progress. While we were still many miles from home, the temperature dropped below 40°F, and a frigid wall of water crashed down upon us from the sky. The drenching rainstorm soaked and chilled us to the bone. We could tell we were beginning to feel the early signs of hypothermia. It became difficult to touch our thumbs to our pinky finger (the hypothermia dexterity test). Being only dressed in thin shirts and pants (some of us in shorts and barefoot), we knew we needed to get out of the cold rain and get warmed up by a fire ASAP.

We quickly found a stand of large conifers that offered some protection from the rain. We did jumping jacks to get the dexterity back into our hands, then we broke off a few dead cedar branches and got to work building a bow drill fire-starting kit. Shortly thereafter we had a roaring fire to warm up by while we waited out the rainstorm. There's an old proverb that says, "Those that chop their own wood are warmed twice," which applies equally well to those that start their own bow drill friction fires!

An hour later we were dried out, warmed up, and the storm had passed. We headed back home after another adventurous day in the field, even more appreciative of the gift of knowing fire-starting skills.

IN THIS CHAPTER YOU WILL LEARN ABOUT:

- The importance of fire

- Types of tinder materials

- The structure of a fire

- The process for building a campfire

- The components of a bow drill friction fire-starting kit

- The process of building your own bow drill kit

- The importance of material selection for friction fire starting

- Step-by-step instructions to create a fire with a bow drill friction fire kit

The Importance of Fire

Fire is number three on the list of survival priorities, and even if you don't spend a lot of time in the outdoors, it can be a very significant skill to have. Sometimes, fire can move from number three to number two or even one on the priority list. This happens when you are in a situation where fire is an essential component to creating a warm and dry shelter or when fire is needed to purify water by boiling.

Fire can perform many survival tasks such as:

- Heat a shelter
- Purify water
- Cook food
- Provide psychological comfort
- Keep wild animals away
- Help rescuers find you via a large smoky campfire that searchers can spot from an aircraft

There are 3 main elements that a fire needs:

- Heat
- Fuel
- Oxygen

Without just one of these, a fire cannot be maintained effectively. Thus, learning to build, start, and sustain a fire, especially in adverse weather, is key.

Building a Fire

Before even thinking about trying to make a spark or lighting a match, gather all the materials needed and prepare them!

Step 1: Gather Tinder

The first material to collect is tinder, which consists of thin, dry, fibrous plant material that will easily catch fire. Examples include certain types of tree bark, dead grasses, and dead flower heads. Gather at least a softball-sized amount of tinder materials, preferably two to three times that volume (especially when it is wet outside).

Tinder Examples:

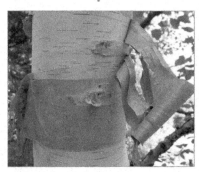

Birch bark is thin and ignites really well, just like paper. But birch is even better than paper because it contains flammable oils. Birch loves the colder regions and grows in a wide variety of topography and soils from rocky ridge tops to peat bogs. You may also find it in other places where people have planted it. You can peel off small sections of the flaky bark without damaging a live tree; however, it's more ethical to harvest the bark from a standing dead tree.

Cedar bark and juniper bark are very similar to one another. These barks light very well when shredded. And because their barks have a woody quality, they will give your fire more stability as the fire begins to grow.

Cedar trees can be found in moist soil, and they grow well in shade. Cedar-dominated forests usually have a lush undergrowth of ferns, as well as a thick carpet of mosses. Junipers can be found in dryer climates both at high and low elevations.

Harvesting small vertical strips (a couple inches wide by a couple feet long) from larger living trees causes injury to the tree, so it is recommended to be done only in emergencies. Harvesting bark from downed or standing dead trees is much more ethical when practicing fire making.

Cottonwood is a lot like birch in its paperlike qualities, and the bark can often be found in large strips when a dead tree breaks apart, making it a great resource!

These trees can be found wherever there is plenty of moisture. Cottonwoods like floodplains and grow well along rivers and streams. They don't do as well in the shade of other species.

Avoid gathering from live trees, as the bark is too moist. Gather the bark of standing dead cottonwood trees since it is dryer and more flammable.

Dry grasses can be found just about anywhere! Collecting a decent amount may take a while, but grass is still a good resource for tinder. If the dead grasses are moist with dew, put them inside your jacket to dry them out over the course of a day.

It really pays off to experiment with different potential tinder materials in your area such as dry, dead inner barks, ferns, grasses, and even flower head fluff from plants such as fireweed and cattail. Try lighting them to see how well they burn. Then, the next time you are out and need a fire, you will know exactly what to look for.

Step 2: Gather Wood

Now that you have tinder for starting the fire, you will need kindling and fuelwood for feeding the fire. It is best to start with really small pieces of wood. Then larger pieces can be added as the fire grows. This is why you need to look for different sizes of kindling to harvest. The key is to slowly graduate to the larger sizes. The more time you spend on gathering appropriate sizes of wood, the better the results. And you will spend less time and energy struggling with a fire that keeps going out.

Hemlock branches

Dead conifer tree twigs are the perfect example of kindling. Gather more than you intend to use on the fire structure because more may be needed later on if the fire is having a difficult time igniting larger pieces of wood. Break off dry and brittle dead branches that are still attached to trees rather than picking up branches off the ground which are often wet. Collect a small armload of dead, dry branches from each of these size groups:

Extra-fine kindling: These branches should be thinner than matchstick diameter and very dry (this size kindling is referred to as the thin-and-wispys)

Fine kindling: Matchstick diameter branches

Regular kindling: Pencil diameter branches

Small fuel sticks: Thicker than pencil diameter but thinner than your thumb

Main fuel sticks: Thicker than thumb diameter. Main fuel sticks are probably the largest size needed for a day hike fire. For a camping fire, gather larger pieces up to about the diameter of your leg.

Extra-fine kindling through main fuel sticks

Step 3: Building the Structure of Your Fire

The Foundation

First, find a good spot to have your fire, making sure not to pick a spot where water might pool. Remove all combustible sticks, leaves, and debris from the ground in about a ten-foot-diameter circle. Also be sure that you are not building your fire on top of tree or shrub roots because the roots can combust and smolder for weeks, later igniting into a forest fire.

If it is wet outside or you are in the snow, make a drier surface on which to build the fire. Lay logs next to each other or use large pieces of bark. Both can work well as a surface.

Branch fire foundation

Bark fire foundation

It is also important to build a ring of stones around the fire pit to prevent it from spreading to the surrounding landscape. This is especially true in dry climates, when it is windy, or in areas with lots of dead, dry plant material on the ground.

The Tinder Bundle

Materials gathered as tinder are mixed together into a moderately compressed, softball-sized sphere called a tinder bundle. This tinder bundle forms the center of the fire structure.

Birch bark strips

Adding cedar bark fibers completes the tinder bundle

Adding the Wood

Next, add the extra-fine kindling, the thin-and-wispys. This layer is very important. Think about the shape of a tipi. There are many other fire structure shapes; however, the tipi struc-

Thin-and-wispys surround the tinder bundle

ture is one of the most effective. The sticks should be meeting at the top and evenly distributed around the tinder bundle. Make sure to leave a little doorway for lighting and feeding the center of the fire. Be sure that this layer of extra-fine kindling is not too loose, keep it fairly tight. I like to straighten the twigs so they are all going in the same direction to form the tipi shape. The tipi shape concentrates the heat so that the fire keeps burning and ignites the larger pieces.

Fuelwood and kindling laid out for efficiency

Continue adding kindling then fuelwood sticks from smallest to largest.
Maintain the shape and structure of
a tipi. Unlike the kindling, the fuelwood pieces should not be packed
too dense or thick. A dense layer of
fuelwood can impede air flow, and
there will not be enough oxygen to
feed the fire.

*Adding larger kindling and small fuel-
wood sticks to the fire tipi structure*

Step 4: Tending the Fire

Now light the tinder bundle through the doorway opening of the tipi
structure with a match, lighter, or ember. The flames should grow and
slowly ignite all the various layers of wood. If conditions are particu-
larly moist, you may need to feed additional small kindling into the
center of the fire to help keep the fire going as it ignites the larger pieces.
Be prepared! Always be sure to have an extra pile of small sticks and
twigs, especially during wet weather conditions. It can also be helpful
to make some wood shavings to have on hand.

At this stage, the fire is like an infant who needs to be fed and taken care of. It also may be necessary to blow on the fire, supplying oxygen to the center to help it catch. Be sure to get down low and blow from the side. Get as close to the base as possible. Move around, try different positions, and adjust the force of the air. Find that perfect spot.

The infant fire waiting to be tended

Once the fire gets going, continue adding fuelwood as needed. If the wood is wet, you can now lay some of the sticks around the base of the tipi to dry them out before adding them to the fire.

Troubleshooting a Reluctant Fire in Wet Conditions

Is your tinder dry?

Even a little moisture can cause trouble. If the tinder is wet, put it in a pocket or elsewhere on your body to dry out over time. You can also carve down into fuelwood branches to get to the driest part of the wood. These wood shavings can be added as an additional layer between the tinder bundle and the extra-fine kindling or used to feed the center of the fire if the tinder bundle burns fast without fully igniting the surrounding sticks.

Is your tinder bundle big enough?

Make sure there is enough woody tinder included in the tinder bundle, such as cedar bark, that burns longer than delicate materials like cattail down. I like to use a large tinder ball of shredded cottonwood, birch, and cedar barks. This helps everything to burn a little slower so the kindling wood has a chance to heat up, dry out, and ignite.

More kindling and blown in oxygen have revived this fire

Are the fuelwood sticks not catching fire?

This can be the result of not having enough kindling, or of having the larger fuel sticks too far away from the center of the fire, or from a limited supply of oxygen. Were enough extra-fine and fine kindling added to your structure? If not, a large cavity may form in the center of the tipi, and the rest of the fuelwood won't catch fire. At this point, the fire can still be saved. Feed the fire more kindling through the doorway of the tipi. After adding more kindling, supply the fire with oxygen by blowing on it. Be careful not to bump the tipi, so it doesn't collapse. Remember to blow from the side rather than from above. If blowing through the door isn't doing the job, find the sweet spot by trying different angles and positions with varying air speed.

Did your tipi collapse?

If the angle of the tipi is too wide or too steep (about 45 degrees is ideal), the structure can collapse. In this case, the fire will struggle. If this happens, just add kindling and fuelwood sticks to reestablish the tipi structure for a successful roaring fire.

Bow Drill Fire Starting

The bow drill is an efficient, simple, and dependable tool for primitive, friction fire starting. With correct materials and good technique, a bow drill will work even in the wettest climates. With a bit of practice, this skill is relatively easy to master. It is the least difficult friction fire-starting technique. Due to its practicality, it is important to learn the bow drill method.

How to Build a Bow Drill Set

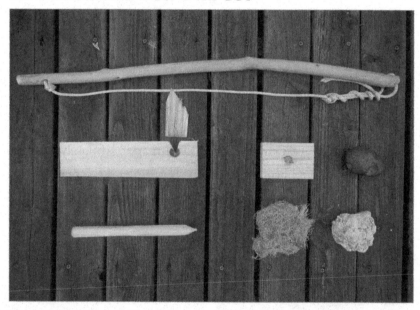

Bow drill fire-starting set. From top to bottom and left to right: bow with string, coal catcher, cedar fireboard, handhold (oak and rock examples), cedar spindle, cedar bark tinder bundle, and optional pine pitch.

Choosing Wood for a Bow Drill Set

Bow drill fire-starting sets are primarily made from the dead dry wood of medium-density tree species such as cottonwood, cedar, alder, willow, aspen, poplar, and many others.

Don't worry if you can't identify a piece of wood. With the **thumb-nail test** it is possible to get by without knowing the species. Using your thumbnail, test whether a dead piece of wood is of the appropriate hardness. Press your thumbnail into the wood; it should make a small visible mark if it is the right density. If the wood is too dense for a bow drill kit, no mark will be visible. If the wood is too soft, the mark will be very deep, or the wood will crumble. The fireboard and spindle should be made of the same wood, or at least a wood of equal density.

When learning bow drill fire starting for the first time, make a kit out of lumber from a hardware store before experimenting with wild wood. Cedar lumber is a great starter material.

Parts of a Bow Drill Set

Spindle or drill: carve a piece of wood or branch so that it becomes a 6- to 10-inch-long cylinder of wood with approximately a thumb diameter. Carve a blunt point on the bottom end to create a large amount of surface area for greater friction and a pencil-tip tapered point on the top end to decrease surface area as much as possible to reduce friction.

Tapered point on the top of a spindle   *Bottom end of a spindle after initial use*

Fireboard: carve a piece of wood large enough to be held with your foot (12 inches long is a good length). It should be the same thickness as the spindle's diameter; be two or more times as wide as the spindle's diameter; and carved flat on top and bottom so as not to wobble.

Two fireboard examples: Top—fireboard made from a cedar branch, Bottom—fireboard made from cedar lumber

Top-rock handhold, Bottom-oak handhold

Handhold or socket: can be a harder material than the spindle. It needs to fit comfortably in your hand and be large enough to keep your fingers clear of the spindle. It can either be carved from a piece of wood, or it can be a rock or bone with a depression in it. The depression must be lubricated. Earwax, bar soap, or waxy conifer needles can be applied to the handhold socket as a lubricant.

Bow: a slightly curved branch, shoulder-to-wrist length, with little or no flex. The diameter and weight need to be a comfortable fit for the user but not so flimsy that the bow breaks under pressure. The type of branch wood used for the bow is not as crucial as with the spindle and fireboard, but it should not be weak or rotten.

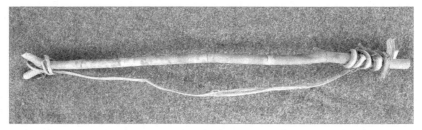

Bow with a cedar rootlet bowstring

Bowstring: a length of cordage made of natural or synthetic materials (such as a cedar rootlet, nettle or dogbane cordage, or a length of shoelace, paracord, or nylon rope) that is approximately shoestring diameter and longer than the bow by at least a few inches on each end.

Cottonwood bark above, pine pitch below

Bow Drill Tinder Bundle: a bundle of fine, fluffy, dry material (such as a combination of shaved cedar bark, dried moss, fireweed fluff, or the inner bark of dead cottonwood) roughly formed into the shape of a bird's nest. It needs to be finer than the rougher tinder bundles made for general fire starting (since it will be igniting from a bow drill coal instead of the flame from a match or lighter). The image shows a tinder bundle of shaved cottonwood bark next to a ball of pine pitch. Small pieces of pitch can be added to the tinder bundle to increase the duration of the flame. In wet climates, the added pitch can be very helpful since you'll need your flame to last longer to dry out wet wood. When learning bow drill for the first time, jute twine can be pulled apart to make a great beginner's tinder bundle.

Preparing the Kit

1. Tie a fixed loop on one end of the bowstring cord (the bowline knot explained next is great for this). Slip the loop over a bow with a forked branch on one end, or carve a notch into the end of the bow, to keep the loop in place. Wrap the other end of the cord through a notch on the other side of the bow, so it can be easily tightened or loosened when necessary.

Forked branch with bowline loop

Cord wrapped at notched end

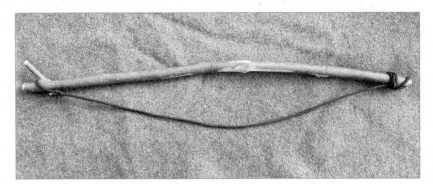
Completed bow

The bowline knot, step-by-step:

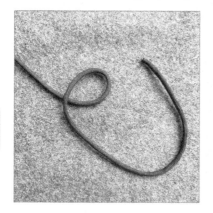

1. Make a rabbit hole (loop over)

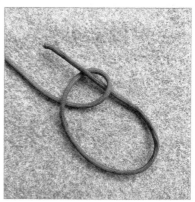

*2. Rabbit comes out of its hole
(under and through loop)*

*3. Rabbit goes around the tree
and back down its hole
(under then over through loop)*

4. Tighten the bowline knot

2. Carve a small starter indent about an inch in from the edge of the fireboard. Assemble your kit (see steps 1 through 6 in the next section, "Body Position and Proper Technique").

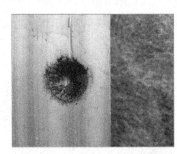
Carve a small indent

3. Using your kit, bow back and forth until you burn the indent into a shallow starter depression (to match the diameter of the spindle) until it is charred just a bit.

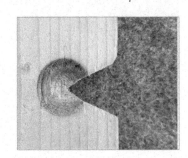
Then burn in a round depression

4. Now carve a notch in the form of a 45 degree pie slice whose point almost reaches the center of the depression. A good guide is to cut the mouth of the notch in line with the two outer edges of the depression as seen in the picture.

Fireboard notch

5. Place a coal catcher, such as a small piece of bark or a dead leaf, underneath the fireboard where the notch is located. As the name implies, this helps to catch any coals that fall from the heated wood dust produced in the notch.

A bark coal catcher in place

6. Proceed as described in the next section.

Body Position, Assembling the Kit, and Proper Technique for Bow Drill Fire Starting

1. Begin by getting into the proper kneeling position by setting your left foot on the fireboard (or if you're left-handed, right foot on the board). Place that foot as close as possible to the starter depression to secure the board. Otherwise, the board will shift as you bow back and forth, causing the wood dust created by the friction of the bow to fall out of the notch before it turns into a coal.

Proper bowing position

2. Put the spindle into the bow by twisting it into the middle of the bow string. The bow string will need to be slightly loose before placing the spindle into it, so that there is enough slack to wrap around the spindle. However, once the spindle is twisted into the bow string, the string needs to become tight, so that the string strongly grips the spindle. See photos on facing page.

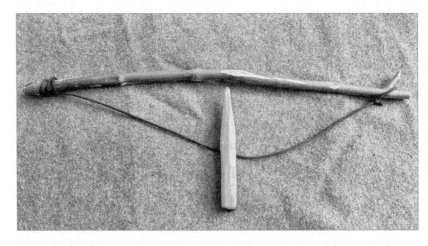

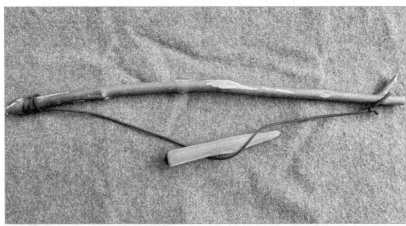

3. Place the spindle, blunt end down, into the fireboard starter depression. Secure the pointed top end of the spindle into the handhold. Make sure the handhold depression is slightly lubricated so that the handhold has minimal friction and does not burn. You can apply a bit of waxy evergreen needles, ear wax, or bar soap into the handhold depression as lubrication. You want all of the friction to be concentrated at the bottom, where the spindle meets the fireboard.

4. Bend your other leg so that you are resting on your knee as shown in the proper bowing position photo. Lean over the bow drill set.

5. Lock your left wrist (or right wrist if left-handed) against the shin of the leg that is holding the board down. If you don't lock your wrist against your shin, the spindle will wobble back and forth as you move the bow, increasing the likelihood of the spindle slipping out of the depression and losing heat rapidly.

6. Keep the spindle vertical in the starter depression and the bow perpendicular to the ground.

7. Begin bowing slowly, using as much of the length of the bow as you can to get started, while applying some downward pressure on the handhold. Then bring the bowing speed up to a steady pace that you can maintain (about one back-and-forth motion per two seconds). The friction and heat caused by the spindle rotating in the fireboard depression combined with the downward pressure creates hot wood dust. This steady pace allows the dust to build up within the notch (see image).

Wood dust in the fireboard notch

8. While maintaining your position, continue bowing steadily and watch for smoke. Also watch to see if the dust is filling up the notch. Seeing smoke and dust filling the notch are good signs. If neither is occurring, increase your bowing speed and/or downward pressure on the handhold.

9. When smoke is visible or the accumulated dust is beginning to turn from a brownish color to black (producing a coal), gradually increase your speed and pressure. As the amount of smoke increases, increase your bowing to a sprinting pace (about two back-and-forth bowing motions per second).

10. When lots of smoke billows from the board, complete ten more sprinting bow strokes and stop. In wetter climates, bow for as long as you possibly can. The goal is to generate the largest coal possible. Larger coals have a better chance of igniting a tinder bundle on wet days.

11. Gently pull your fireboard away from the pile of dust and observe it closely. Is the dust pile still smoking? If yes, continue to step 12. If not, go back to step 1.

12. Let the coal breathe and grow for a moment and watch for darkening and glowing in the dust pile. Do not blow on it or fan it with your hand. In fact, if it is too windy, give the pile a bit of shelter.

13. Grab the tinder bundle and double check that it is ready to accept the coal. If needed tease it apart to create as much surface area as possible. Then fluff it up into a bird's nest shape with a small cavity in the middle for the coal to sit. Aim for a medium density of fibers. A bundle that is too loose will not have enough material close to the coal to ignite. A bundle that is too dense will not allow enough oxygen to get to the coal.

14. Once the coal reaches the point of being a visible, red-hot ember in the core of your dust, position the coal catcher with the coal right over the tinder bundle and gently tip the coal into the nest. Then

carefully cradle the tinder material around the coal. Raise the tinder bundle above your face and blow it gently into flame. Slow, deep breaths are better than fast, shallow breaths. Also, hold your face at least 3 to 4 inches away from the bundle so as not to dampen the tinder with

Holding lit bundle with fingertips

your breath. Be sure to hold the tinder bundle from below with your fingers. Cupping the bundle all around prevents oxygen flow and can cause you to get burned once the tinder ignites.

15. Place the flaming bundle into the tipi fire structure that you have prepared beforehand and continue to blow on it until the flame jumps up to larger materials.

And that's the magic of friction fire starting!

CHAPTER SUMMARY

- Fire can become the second or even first survival priority if the situation requires it to make a warm enough shelter or if fire is required to boil water for purification.

- When starting a fire with natural materials, collect a variety of dry tinder materials and various sizes of kindling and fuelwood to make a tipi-shaped fire structure.

- When a lighter or matches or any other modern fire-starting equipment is not available, the bow drill is the least difficult friction technique for starting fires with natural materials found in the wilderness.

CHAPTER 5

Wild Survival Foods

The longer a survival situation lasts, the more important food becomes. This point is illustrated in longer-term survival scenarios. One situation that comes to mind is the lost boys of Ata who survived on a deserted island for over a year. The importance of food is also apparent on the survival TV show Alone. The Alone contestants who are able to continue surviving beyond a few weeks are those that successfully obtain wild foods. So once you have your shelter, water, and fire systems in place, it is time to focus your efforts on harvesting wild foods.

With plants being the most readily available survival food group, it's important to start with learning plant identification skills. Never eat a plant if you are not 100 percent certain of its identity. Again, from personal experience, I can't emphasize enough how important proper plant identification skills are to your safety.

I've spent most of my career teaching wilderness survival skills to college-age students. I encourage students to *continue practicing wilderness skills outside of formal class times and field trips. It's always great to see excited students form extracurricular groups based on topics of shared interest.*

One school year early in my career, in the spring of 2001, a group of students formed an informal wild edible plants potluck group to take place on weekends. I was invited and attended several meetings. Each student would bring different dishes they had made from various wild edible plants they were studying. It was a fantastic opportunity to share new recipes and eat preparations of wild foods like stinging nettle soup, dandelion fritters, and pine needle tea.

On one such occasion, one of the students brought a dish of steamed cattail shoots. Not long after taking the first bites someone asked, "What hot spice was added to the recipe?" The reply was, "None." Then another person remarked, "My mouth is burning is yours?" Several others replied, "Yes, my mouth is burning too!" I inspected the dish and asked the cook a few plant ID questions. I quickly came to the conclusion that this student had accidentally misidentified yellow flag iris for cattail. Luckily for everyone, yellow flag iris is only moderately toxic and just caused irritation and digestive discomfort, rather than anything more serious. The situation could have been much worse if the misidentification was within the wild carrot plant family.

This illustrates the fact that, no matter how excited you may be to start eating wild plants, you must first solidify your plant identification skills. Cross reference with multiple field guides and consult with an experienced forager if you have any bit of uncertainty. Practice your plant identification skills often and bring wild edibles into your daily life. Not only is it fun, you'll be ready if you need them in an emergency.

IN THIS CHAPTER YOU WILL LEARN ABOUT:

- The basics of plant Identification

- Hazards associated with foraging for wild plants

- Common wild edible plants found across North America

- The importance of protein and fats in extended survival situations

- Tools and techniques for capturing small game

- Hazards associated with eating small animals

Finding wild foods is a key wilderness survival skill, especially for longer-term survival situations that extend beyond a few days. Plants are often more abundant and more easily harvested than wild game since wild game can be elusive. Utilizing wild foods takes a degree of naturalist knowledge. Proper plant identification is paramount.

To find edible plants, you must have some knowledge of where they grow—in terms of geographic range—as well as what conditions they grow in and how to differentiate them from any poisonous look-alikes. You must not only know what a plant is and how to use it, but also at what time of year it can be used, which parts to harvest, and how to process it. It is best to avoid harvesting from areas that may be contaminated by pollution such as roadsides. Also avoid harvesting any plants that are rare, threatened, or endangered unless your life is truly at risk. When practicing, stick to common, abundant species. Growing your plant knowledge takes time and practice however it's easy to get started by choosing several common wild edible plants in your area to get to know well.

Plant Identification— Look at the Parts

When attempting to identify a plant, it helps to look carefully at all the available parts and their characteristics. Take photos of the plant to bring home, or bring plant identification guidebooks into the field. The most important parts to look at are the flowers, branching patterns, and leaves. Determining the flower, branching, and leaf types (along with other features) will help you use plant identification field guides to narrow down options and positively identify an unknown plant. This chart explains some of the basic flower, branching, and leaf types.

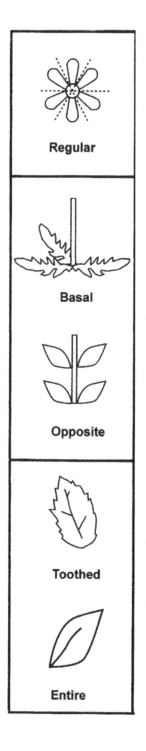

Regular

Basal

Opposite

Toothed

Entire

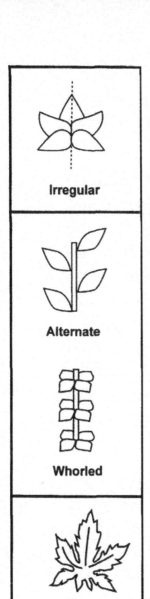

Flower Type
(overall flower shape):

Regular-having a shape that is symmetrical multiple ways

Irregular-having a shape that is symmetrical only one way

Indistinguishable-having flower parts that are too small to see

Branching Type
(leaf arrangement):

Basal-leaves only growing at the base of the plant

Alternate-leaves arranged singly along the stem

Opposite-leaves growing in pairs directly across from each other along the stem

Whorled-groups of three or more leaves growing out around a branch

Leaf Type
(leaf edges):

Toothed-the leaf edge has shallow indentations that are pointed or wavy

Lobed-the leaf edge has one or more deep indentations

Entire-the leaf edge is smooth/straight

Divided-the leaf is divided into separate parts called leaflets.

When you combine the flower, branching, and leaf type with other prominent features observed (such as flower color, number of petals, leaf texture, thorns, etc.) you will be equipped with excellent information for identifying a mystery plant in good field guides.

For plant identification books, we recommend using *Newcomb's Wildflower Guide* (for its systematic identification key) in conjunction with a quality regional photographic guide such as *Plants of the Pacific Northwest Coast*. Using the combination of *Newcomb's* with a regional plant identification field guide to cross reference information is a reliable approach to identifying mystery plants. Good regional plant identification guides often contain numerous color photographs, a dichotomous key, and are organized by plant family or flower color. You can also double check your identification with an experienced wild foods forager. Once a plant has been positively identified, you can then explore the details for harvesting, processing, and adding that plant into recipes.

Some students have asked about plant identification apps for smartphones. We've found that they are not yet effective at positively identifying plants. Sometimes they can provide a list of possibilities that may include the plant you're attempting to identify, but oftentimes it's not there. And they don't help you become self-sufficient with your own observations and identification skills.

Not until you have positively identified a plant with certainty, researched how and when to use it, made sure it is a common/abundant plant (not a rare plant), know that you are not allergic to it, and have determined that the area is not contaminated, can you then consider harvesting and consuming the plant. When harvesting for practice (not a survival emergency), you'll also want to be sure to harvest ethically. This means only taking a small portion of the plant to ensure there is plenty left for wildlife and to allow the plant population to continue. A good rule for harvesting berries or leaves is to never take more than one third of the berries/leaves on a given plant. If you need to harvest the entire plant or its root, a good rule is to never harvest more than one per group of twenty specimens.

All of this will become second nature as you follow the amazing journey of using wild edible plants!

Wild Edible Plants to Start With

Some wild edible plants are found far and wide. It is useful to get familiar with common, widespread species as a starting point for building a knowledge base useful for wilderness survival.

Below are some of the best plants to get to know as a source of food for survival.

Cattail *(Typha latifolia)*

 This wide-ranging species, and other *Typha* species, is a wealth of food and utilitarian resources. The rhizomes, young shoots, immature flowers, and pollen are all choice edibles. The leaves of the cattail are long, spongy in cross-section, and often grow in abundance. They can be used to construct containers, mats, shelters, bedding, and more. The fluffy late-season seed heads, also known as cattail down, provide excellent insulation for use in clothing, bedding, and pillows.

This cattail down can also be added to tinder bundles to help improve flammability. Be sure not to misidentify yellow iris for cattail.

Dandelion *(Taraxacum officinale)*

This member of the aster family was originally introduced to North America as a food and medicine. The dandelion has multiple edible parts, including: flowers, roots, young leaves, and flower buds. This is a highly nutritious, bitter green that is worth eating. Dandelion greens are least bitter in springtime, before they flower. Younger leaves in general are a better-tasting choice for eating. If you have a latex allergy, you may also be allergic to dandelion.

Oaks (*Quercus* species and *Lithocarpus* species)

There are a diverse number of oak species across the world. They are a vital part of the landscapes in which they grow and feed many species. The acorns of all oaks are edible. Some require more processing than others. Wherever they were found in abundance, oaks were generally utilized as a staple food source by hunter-gatherers. Acorns must be shelled and boiled in several changes of water, or they can be leached in a stream for several days to remove the bitter tannins, which can also be toxic. They can then be eaten as is, mashed into porridge, or turned into a flour.

Blackberries and Raspberries (*Rubus* species)

This group of berry-producing plants in the rose family is widespread and easy to identify. They generally fruit in the summertime, but the flowers in late spring are edible as are the young delicate spring shoots.

Pines (*Pinus* species)

Pines are found all over the world. These trees have long needles in bundles of one to six. Pines produce woody cones which contain edible seeds. The needles also make a beverage, rich in vitamin C, when

put into hot water. It is important not to boil them, however, as this releases turpentine and can cause discomfort or nausea. The cambium (living tissue) layer on the trunk of pines is edible, though best cooked. It can be harvested by breaking off the outer bark and scraping the cambium with a knife or rock. Be mindful to not ring the tree (do not remove bark in a complete circle around the trunk) if you are harvesting cambium as this will certainly kill the tree. Ethically, it is best to limit cambium harvesting to trees that have been recently blown down in a windstorm or trees you intend to take down, since cambium harvesting can open up a wound that allows disease or insects to come in and kill the tree.

Stinging Nettle
(Urtica dioica)

This wide-ranging species is often first discovered by the unwary when they brush up against its stinging hairs. You might be surprised to learn that this unfriendly plant is an excellent food. The young shoots (six to twelve inches tall), younger leaves on mature plants, and seeds in the late summer are all edible. The greens are best eaten steamed or boiled to remove the stinging quality. The seeds of nettles are good eaten raw or cooked with other grains into a porridge. Incidentally, the fibers from the stalk can be turned into strong cordage.

Wild Spinach
(Lamb's Quarters)
(Chenopodium album)

This edible wild green is one of the most widespread weeds in the world. The leaves, bud clusters, growing tips, and seeds are all edible. The small toothed arrowhead-shaped leaves often look like they are covered in a white powder. This white coating is tiny, wax-like crystals that can help you to properly identify this delicious wild green.

Common Plantain
(*Plantago major*)

This edible green is a common weed species in lawns, pastures, trail sides, and meadows. It has large, basal leaves that are oblong. The major veins in the leaves are pronounced, contain

string-like fibrous material inside them, and converge towards the tip of the leaf. The young leaves are edible, as are older leaves when cooked, and the edible seed is high in dietary fiber. Plantain is also an excellent medicinal plant, used externally in a poultice form for bruises, burns, and bee stings. The narrow-leaved plantain can be used the same way.

QUESTIONS ABOUT GATHERING WILD EDIBLES

At Alderleaf, we get hundreds of questions from students regarding wild edibles every year. Rather than trying to answer all of them here, I've selected the three most asked questions, which happen to be perhaps the most important ones to ask!

Where do I start?

There is such a wide variety of wild edible plants out there that it is easy to be overwhelmed. Start learning those that are really common and readily available where you live (such as in local parks). There is a good chance that several of the species mentioned here, such as dandelion and lamb's quarters, may even be growing in your backyard. Start with five to ten species and learn everything you can about them from multiple field guides (both identification field guides and wild edible plants books). As your confidence grows with those few plants, start expanding to new ones. Take it slow. If you have food allergies, avoid wild plants that are closely related to food plants you are allergic to. Tom Elpel's book *Botany in a Day* is a great resource for learning which plants are related to each other by being in the same family group. Also, consider taking wild edible plants courses in your area. Nothing beats having an experienced wild foods forager teaching you directly about the plants around you.

There are so many edible plant books, which is best for me?

This really depends on where you live and on which wild edible plants you want to focus. Here are some resources I highly recommend:

- *Edible Wild Plants: Wild Foods from Dirt to Plate* by John Kallas
- *The Forager's Harvest* and *Nature's Garden* both by Samuel Thayer
- *Discovering Wild Plants* by Janice Schofield
- *The Forager's Guide to Wild Foods* by Nicole Apelian

If I can't identify a plant for certain, should I eat it?

No. Do not eat it. Although many wild plants are edible or harmless if eaten, a few are fatally poisonous. Others can cause severe, though usually temporary, discomfort. You must be thorough and cautious in your identification process. If you are uncertain of a plant's identity, even after cross checking it in multiple reliable field guides, then contact an experienced wild plants forager.

Practical Survival Protein

In most survival situations, the primary source of food is plant matter. Plant matter is an excellent source of fiber and vitamins, and it is quite easy to procure if you have a good grasp of species identification. The one thing that many wild plants are not as good at is providing abundant calories. Succulent plant matter is quickly digested by your stomach and may not provide enough energy for the tasks of survival.

Proteins and fats are the food components that give your body a good source of long-term metabolic energy. Hunting large game is generally unpractical for most survival situations. However, there are easier ways to acquire protein and fats in a survival situation.

Hunting Small Game: Tools of the Trade

Many small animals can be effectively hunted with two tools: a stick and a rock. In a survival situation, *after* you have satisfied all of your other survival priorities and acquired some basic plants foods, you can start thinking about hunting small game. Once you've taken care of your basic survival necessities, you can carry a rabbit stick and a few golf-ball-sized rocks whenever you're out gathering more firewood or water.

Rabbit Stick

This tool consists of a branch broken or cut to be about as long as your arm from shoulder to wrist. It should have some heft to it when you swing it but not so heavy as to be unwieldy or uncomfortable to carry or throw. This is your club for catching small animals at close range. It can also be thrown overhand, or sideways from the hip.

Rock

This tool is a round or slightly oblong stone about as big as a golf ball. You can keep a few in your pockets as you walk around and use them to throw at birds or small mammals during an emergency survival situation.

To practice your accuracy, you can set up targets in your backyard for throwing rabbit sticks and rocks, similar to archery practice.

Species to Consider: Vertebrates

Certain species of snakes, frogs, birds, and fish are excellent prey animals to target in survival situations. Be sure to remove the guts and skin, and cook the meat thoroughly. Also, get to know your local fish and game laws before capturing any wildlife.

Snakes

Snakes are great prey in many parts of the country because they are fairly predictable in their routines. They are ectothermic, meaning that they rely on their environment to maintain their body temperature. Snakes are reliably found at mid morning, basking in open sunlit areas, especially in rocky locations.

Many parts of the country have venomous snake species, so be sure to familiarize yourself with them before hunting snakes. Do not attempt to kill a venomous snake. In a survival situation, it is not worth the risk. Garter snakes (*Thamnophis sp.*)

can be found in a wide range of habitats and climates and are nonvenomous. They can be caught by hand or pinned with a stick while you swiftly remove the head.

Birds

Birds are another great source of survival protein. Ducks and other waterfowl can be hunted since they spend most of their time on the ground or on the water. Ground feeding birds can be another good prey item. Some areas of the country have game birds like grouse, pheasants, and turkeys. These species are often found foraging on the ground or roosting in low trees.

Bird nests can also provide a reliable source of protein in spring. If you happen to be in a survival situation during spring, look for clumps of sticks, moss, grasses, feathers, and mud in shrubs or low trees. Eggs can be eaten just like you would a chicken egg. Baby birds can also be consumed in survival emergencies.

Fish

If you happen to be near a body of water, fish can be utilized as a great source of protein. A simple fish trap can be made from sticks or rocks stuck into the mud at the edge of a lake shore. You can also catch minnows by herding them into a shallow pool and then using a t-shirt wrapped over sticks as a makeshift net to scoop them up.

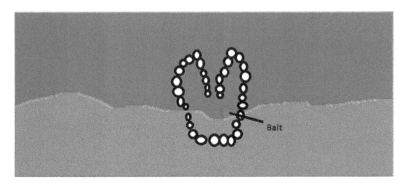

A simple rock fish trap

Frogs

Bullfrogs, for example, can be found all over North America and are considered an invasive species in many areas of the country. They also happen to be a reliable source of meat. Bullfrogs can be found near bodies of water and can be identified at a distance by their distinctive call, which has been compared to the roar of a bull. They can be caught by hand or with a long, sharpened stick fashioned as a frog gig or fish spear. Again, proper identification skills are key, as some frog species and most toad species are toxic.

Species to Consider: Invertebrates

In many parts of the world certain species of insects and snails are considered delicacies. In a survival situation, they can be consumed as a quick and easy source of protein. A reliable safe practice is to add insects to soups or cook them in other ways prior to eating them. This will kill any parasites that could be living inside the insect.

Grubs

Beetles (*Coleoptera*) go through a larval stage early in life. These larval beetles are commonly referred to as grubs and look like short fat fleshy white worms. They can be found under logs, in rotting tree stumps, and other forest debris. Grubs taste very plain, but around 60 percent of their body is made of protein, the other 40 percent being composed of fats.

Grasshoppers and Crickets

The *Orthoptera* genus includes crickets, grasshoppers, and locusts. They tend to have large, fleshy bodies and crunchy wings and legs. They can be eaten whole or stripped of the head and legs before consumption. They have a pleasant nutty, almost shrimp-like flavor that improves with cooking. They are also loaded with protein.

Earthworms

These invertebrates are found all over the world. They contain as much protein by volume as eggs or milk. They also contain significant amounts of calcium, iron, and potassium. They are

primarily active in wet soils and are more often found near the surface at night or in rainy weather.

Snails

Considered a delicacy in France, these gastropods can be eaten cooked. The shell is inedible. They are generally found in moist temperate climates and are more often seen during rainy weather. Be sure to cook them thoroughly to kill any parasites they may be carrying.

Species to Avoid

Hunting for survival protein follows the same rules as foraging for plants. Learn identification skills. There are some animals that are toxic. Get to know the species in your local area so that you know what to avoid.

For instance, the rough-skinned newt (*Taricha granulosa*), pictured right, is extremely poisonous if eaten, causing death within hours.

Rough-skinned newt

Most North American toads are also poisonous if eaten. Avoid eating toads.

Bright colors on insects are an indication of toxicity. Avoid eating bugs with bright colors such as lady bugs and clown millipedes.

With these few exceptions, the outdoors is full of wild survival foods.

CHAPTER SUMMARY

- Plant identification is one of the most important skills for getting started with foraging.

- Never consume a plant or animal that you have not first identified with 100 percent certainty.

- Learn about the most common and abundant wild edible plants in your area, then expand your knowledge out to other species.

- *After* securing shelter and water, you can prepare yourself for hunting small game.

- Small prey items such as birds, fish, frogs, snakes, and invertebrates are easier to acquire than large game in a survival situation and provide a source of protein, fat, and calories.

N
20
40
60
EAST DECLINATION
80
E
100
120
140
160
S
200
220
240
260
W
280
WEST DECLINATION
300
320
340

CHAPTER 6

Preparation & Prevention

Many survival situations can be avoided through good preparation and prevention, such as carrying a survival kit and knowing how to navigate. However, many survival situations are due to an unexpected emergency or to lost, destroyed, or forgotten equipment. That's why it's important to learn primitive survival skills!

In July of 2015, I was interviewed by Seattle's King 5 News when the epic survival story of sixteen-year-old Autumn Veatch became public. She was flying home to Bellingham, WA, from Montana with her grandparents in their small plane when the plane went down and crashed in the North Cascades. Autumn survived the fiery wreck with bruises and burns; however, her grandparents didn't make it. Any first aid kits, tools, or survival kits that may have been in the plane were destroyed by the blaze.

Autumn stayed by the wreck for a day or two, hoping searchers would arrive. However, no help came. Autumn didn't have any survival training to fall back on; how-

ever, she remembered a few survival tips from TV programs she had watched with her father years before. She remembered that if searchers don't know where to look for you, or if days go by without anyone finding you, you need to find your own way out of the wilderness. She remembered the tip to go downhill until you find a stream, then to follow the water downstream until you get back to civilization.

Autumn made her way downhill out of the mountains. She found a stream and followed it downstream, scaling down several waterfalls along the way, until the stream joined a larger creek. The water looked dirty, and Autumn didn't have any purification tools. She decided not to drink it, since she didn't want to get too sick to keep hiking. She slept overnight on a sandbar along the creek, huddled in a sweatshirt, without shelter or fire. It was so cold that she didn't get any sleep. But the next day, Autumn kept following the creek downhill, determined to make it out to civilization. Eventually, the creek crossed a hiking trail that led her down to Highway 20. Two hikers found her there and brought her to Brewster, WA, where she was treated for dehydration and burns at a local hospital.

Autumn's story is amazing and hopeful. She did her best with the circumstances in which she found herself. When the going got so tough that she believed she wouldn't make it, she thought about her family and friends. Those thoughts motivated her to keep going. The will to live is a powerful factor in many survival emergencies. Despite not having any formal survival training, she kept her wits about her and persevered. Unlike so many others, Autumn made it out alive and returned to her family.

Autumn's story illustrates a less common survival situation where navigating out of the wilderness is preferred to surviving in place until help arrives. Had she stayed by the plane, there was no guarantee that she wouldn't succumb to hypothermia or dehydration, especially if searchers didn't find the wreck. She made good choices, had luck on her side, and ultimately made it out alive without special equipment and with only knowing a few survival tips. Many aren't as fortunate. Imagine how her situation would have been vastly better with primitive survival skills or a survival kit on hand.

IN THIS CHAPTER YOU WILL LEARN ABOUT:

- Different kinds of survival equipment
- Survival kits and how to assemble one
- Concerns when choosing equipment for a survival kit
- The importance of navigation skills
- Compasses and how they work
- Celestial bodies and landforms and how to use them in navigation
- Walking out to civilization and how to do it safely

Survival Kits

A good survival kit is extremely helpful for both aiding in and preventing wilderness emergency situations. It contains tools that allow you to meet your needs faster and can help keep you safe. Having some gear handy can also help combat feelings of anxiety or fear that may arise during outdoor emergencies and can also increase feelings of empowerment. Survival kits come in many varieties, from pocket-sized tins all the way up to giant bugout bags. We recommend keeping a small survival kit in your daypack, a medium-sized kit in your car, and a larger kit at home.

What is needed?

When putting together a survival kit, first think about what your needs are. What is the climate and ecology of the wilderness area? What kind of background knowledge or skills do you have? And, how portable does your kit need to be for this application?

What should be included?

There are many options for what goes into a survival kit. In choosing the contents of a kit, the most important things to consider are the survival priorities:

1. Shelter

2. Water

3. Fire

4. Food

Ideally, each tool in your kit should be able to satisfy multiple priorities, and each priority should be supported by multiple tools.

Another perspective on survival kits is to think in terms of the "Eleven Systems" (which is modified from the Mountaineers' "Ten Essentials for Hiking"):

System	Potential Gear for a Kit	Primitive Alternatives
1. Shelter	Bivvy, tarp, blanket	Natural shelters
2. Water	Filters, water bottles	Burned-bowl rock boiling
3. Fire Starting	Lighter, matches, fuel	Friction fire-starting kit
4. Extra Food	Protein bars	Foraged wild food
5. Navigation	Map, compass, GPS	Aidless navigation skills
6. First Aid	First aid kit	Medicinal wild plants
7. Extra Clothing	Compact extra layers	Bark, debris, hides
8. Illumination	Flashlight, headlamp	Campfire
9. Tools	Knife, duct tape, rope	Stone tools, pitch, rootlets
10. Sun Protection	Sunscreen, hat	Mud, clay
11. Communication	Cell phone, emergency whistle, signaling mirror, SPOT device	Large, emergency signal fire with lots of smoke

Fundamental Survival Kit Tools:

The following tools are considered essential components of an effective, versatile survival kit. These tools address the top priorities for wilderness survival.

Compass

A compass can help with navigating out to safety. It can also prevent a survival situation from happening before it even starts. A compass can prevent hikers from getting lost but only if combined with a map or a healthy familiarity with the surrounding wilderness area.

Knife

A knife can be used to split firewood, cut branches for a shelter, fashion a bow drill kit, skin animals, harvest plants, and carve other tools out of wood. A good survival knife has the following features:

- It is full tang (the metal of the blade extends into the handle as one piece)

- It has a fixed blade (folding knives can be susceptible to damage and breaking)

- The blade is high carbon tempered steel (this allows the blade to bend instead of break)

- The handle is comfortable in your hand

Fire Starting Tools

Fire can provide heat for a shelter, purify water, cook food, and help to make other tools and containers. Always include at least two different ways to start a fire. Usually these are a lighter, waterproof matches, or a ferrocerium rod (also known as a firesteel). Having at least two different fire-starting tools increases the likelihood that one of them will work in a given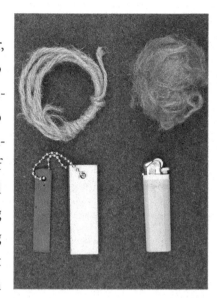

situation. Fire-starting aids such as Vaseline-soaked cotton balls and dry tinder material should also be included.

Wool Blanket or Mylar Blanket

This handy piece of gear helps to satisfy the first survival priority: shelter. It can also be used as a carrying device for debris or firewood. Wool retains its insulation even when wet and is also antimicrobial and fire resistant. A Mylar blanket (commonly referred to as a *space blanket*) is a highly reflective sheet of plastic that helps retain natural body heat. It can also be used to reflect heat away from the body in a sunny environment.

Metal Water Bottle

This versatile piece of gear can be used to carry, store, and collect water. Metal bottles can also be used to boil water for purification. Steel water bottles are best used for this purpose. Aluminum water bottles can also be used, but they carry health risks if used to boil water long-term. A bottle of warm water can also be held between clothing layers to help maintain body heat at night in a shelter.

Emergency Whistle

A lightweight, ultra-loud whistle can be used to signal for help. A whistle carries *much* farther than a shout and won't tax the lungs as much. Three blasts in a row is the universal signal for SOS; however, any kind of whistle being blown in the backcountry will attract attention.

Kit Size

A barebones, ultralight survival kit should have at least the first three items (a compass, a quality knife, and two ways to start fire). A heavier, but still quite portable kit can be made from all six items.

Additional Items

Anything beyond the previous six items will add an element of comfort to a survival experience and increase the possibility of surviving longer in the backcountry. However, additional items will also add bulk and weight to a survival kit, so items should be chosen with careful consideration. A large, heavy kit has a higher chance of being left home instead of being brought into the outdoors.

Water Purification

Water is a high survival priority. Surface water that is not purified can carry harmful parasites or bacteria that can seriously hinder chances of survival if a hiker is lost and alone. A water purification aid (beyond using a metal water bottle to boil water) can come in handy while on the move.

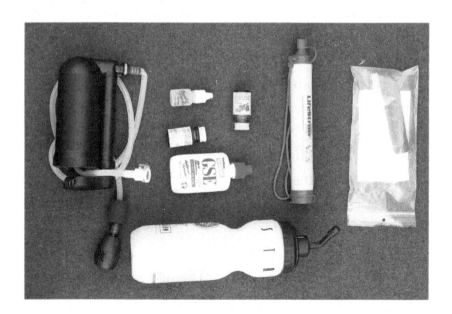

Purification systems can take the form of commercial backpacking water filtration device or a vial of water purification tablets. There are also UV-light-based water purification devices out on the market, though they require batteries and very clear water to function correctly.

Cordage

This is another highly versatile item that can be used to support multiple survival priorities. The most economical and reliable cordage material for a simple survival kit is 550 parachute cord (also known as paracord). Cordage can be used to lash a shelter together, as the string for a bow drill friction fire-starting kit, or used for snares, among many other things. The uses for cordage are limited only by the imagination.

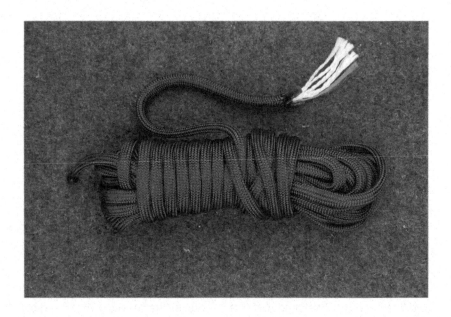

First Aid Kit

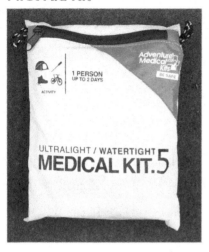

Medical aid and attention can be much farther away in the wilderness than in civilization. A first aid kit is very helpful for patching up minor wounds, and it is especially important for guides who are leading a group as part of an organization or official outing. Every person's first aid kit will vary according to their specific skill level and needs. It is important for the user to know how to apply the materials in the kit.

A good, basic first aid kit will contain the following:

- Basic adhesive strip bandages (BandAid® brand)
- A roll of medical gauze
- A pressure bandage (Ace Wraps™)
- Anti-inflammatory pain killers (ibuprofen)
- Antihistamine medication (over-the-counter allergy medication)
- Medical tape and/or duct tape
- Alcohol wipes or iodine

A first aid kit with the above items will be small, relatively compact, and should be sufficient for anything that does not call for hospitalization. Other items to consider are extra medications for any chronic illnesses or personal health issues, an epinephrine pen if you have severe allergies, or simple herbal salves and remedies for minor medical needs.

Tarp

This tool helps to secure shelter, the first survival priority. It can keep rain off the body, provide shelter from the sun, or be used to carry or gather water and other supplies. Many companies produce backpacking ponchos that double as serviceable tarps. A tarp for a survival kit should be no more than eight feet by eight feet in dimension. Avoid heavy utility tarps that are frequently sold in supermarkets. Opt instead for a lightweight camping tarp found at most sporting goods stores.

Light

A headlamp or small flashlight can be a great tool to include in a survival kit. A light allows movement and activity at night and can be used to signal rescuers. A light can also provide a great deal of comfort and raise morale at night, especially if the prospect of being alone in the dark is frightening. Be sure to use a fire as the main light source around camp at night or the headlamp/flashlight batteries will be quickly depleted!

Extra Food

Food is a low survival priority, but including a small amount of emergency food in a kit is a good idea. This is especially important for those who have a history of experiencing hypoglycemia (low blood sugar).

The best food items to choose have the following characteristics.

- High caloric density
- Nonperishable
- No cooking required

Protein bars are a good choice. One or two bars are sufficient for a personal survival kit.

Tools

A hatchet, machete, or portable folding saw can make life easier while operating in dense brushy terrain or processing a lot of large logs into fire wood. These tools also tend to be prohibitively heavy for a backpacking survival kit. Light repair tools, such as a small roll of duct tape and a compact sewing kit make good, compact additions to a survival kit.

Several additional items to consider include a compact fishing kit (line and hooks), sunscreen, a signaling mirror, and extra layers of clothing (e.g., a hat and packable set of rain gear).

All of these survival kit items can be found at outdoor sporting goods stores or online.

Survival Navigation

Many wilderness survival stories begin with a person getting lost in the woods. By taking preventive action and by using appropriate knowledge and skills, the possibility of getting lost can be minimized. Similarly, navigation skills can be used to find your way out of the woods when in a situation where rescuers won't be looking for you or a search is called off after a week.

How to Prevent Getting Lost

By becoming familiar with the following aspects of survival navigation you can significantly decrease the chances of becoming lost and increase the possibility of finding the way back to the trail or civilization.

The Big Picture
(using major landforms to help you navigate)

Study maps of the local area. Start with your city or town. While out running errands, get into the habit of picturing where you would be on a map. By keeping the big picture in mind, you will become familiar with a bird's eye view of the world. Before beginning a wilderness trek, study a topographical map ahead of time to identify major landmarks. Most wilderness areas are bounded by highways or rivers. Keep these landmarks in mind. They can act as points of reference or may represent potential places of rescue.

Celestial Bodies

The sun, moon, and stars can be used as absolute points of reference to find the four cardinal directions.

SUN

Because of the earth's rotation, our sun rises in an easterly direction and sets in a westerly direction that varies seasonally and with regard to latitude. Near midday in the northern hemisphere, it is due south (which means shadows cast by the sun at midday will point due north).

MOON

The moon also rises in an easterly direction and sets in a westerly direction that varies seasonally and with regard to latitude.

STARS

The North Star (Polaris) is directly above Earth's North Pole (albeit many light years away). Find this reference point in the night sky by locating the Big Dipper (Ursa Major constellation). The two stars on the front of the dipper's scoop point toward the North Star.

Form an imaginary line through these two stars to create a pointer toward Polaris, the North Star.

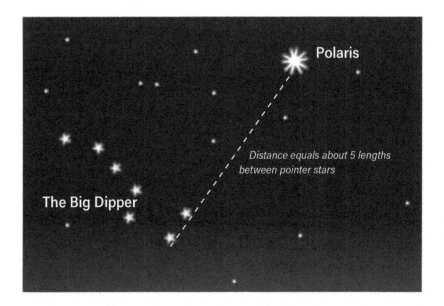

Polaris

Distance equals about 5 lengths between pointer stars

The Big Dipper

Trail Blazing

When traveling off trail, create a series of markers that can be followed if it is necessary to go back the way you came. The cairn is the most common marker used by hikers. It consists of a small stack of rocks balanced on top of one another. This marker has the advantage of being made of natural materials and of being conspicuous on the landscape; however, cairns can be hidden by snowfall. Another trailblazing method is to mark trees as they are passed, either by breaking limbs or cutting away a small piece of bark. This method is relatively invasive, and the blazes may blend in with storm damage. Yet another trailblazing option is to tie pieces of bright-colored flagging tape onto branches periodically along the way in. These flags can then be followed and taken down on the way out.

Song-lining

This is the technique of making up a story based on the most prominent landmarks or distinct objects that you pass along the way to your destination. It is similar to trail blazing, but instead of physical markers, mental markers are created for landmarks. Finding the way back is as simple as telling the story in reverse. Many indigenous cultures used this technique.

Back-Tracking

A skilled tracker may not need to leave blazes or cairns. Footprints and trails of disturbance often stand out to a tracker's eye. This makes back-tracking another method of finding the way back by reversing the way in, especially in snowy or sandy conditions where tracks are most visible.

Map and Compass

Be prepared to navigate when going into the wilderness. A map and compass are the most important tools for navigation. Bring a topographical map of the local area and a baseplate compass even when just out on a day hike. Plan out which routes will be used and look for landmarks that will help you gauge your location on the map.

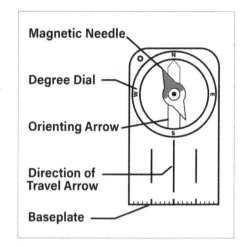

Baseplate compass

Orienting a Compass

The most basic function of a compass is to locate magnetic north. In many situations, this will be a good enough gauge to get a general sense of direction. Simply hold the compass flat in front of you and turn your whole body until the red side of the magnetic needle is pointing directly away from you.

Once you know which direction is north, you'll also know which direction is east, south, and west. Orienting to these cardinal directions can help you avoid getting lost and help you navigate to safety, especially when paired with a map. To use a map effectively, it helps to orient it in accordance with the terrain it represents. All maps (unless otherwise noted) assume that the top edge of the map is north. Using a compass, locate north, orient the map in that direction and then figure out where nearby landmarks are in relation to you. The combination of a map and compass is a powerful tool to help prevent you from getting lost. Check out the *Supplementary Resources* at the end of the book for more in-depth compass skills instruction, including the concept of declination and reading a topographic map.

How to Remedy Being Lost

Getting lost can still happen. There is no doubt that being lost ranks at the top of most outdoors enthusiasts' list of fears. However, combined with basic survival knowledge, the navigation techniques above become a powerful skill set to enable a lost person to return to civilization safely. Below are recommendations for the two most common scenarios.

Staying Put

If someone knows where to look for you, then stay where you are. This is why it is essential to tell someone where you are going in the wilderness and when you will be back. If you get lost in that area, it will be a simpler matter for rescuers to find you. A moving person is significantly harder for searchers to locate. Another hazard of being on the move while in a survival situation is that it is much harder to take care of the survival priorities of shelter, water, fire, and food.

Walking Out

If you don't tell anyone where you are going or when you expect to return and then become completely lost in a wilderness area, your chances of being found by searchers are much smaller. Additionally, most searches are called off after a week of effort, so if you are sheltering in place and no rescue teams appear within a week you will likely need to navigate out on your own. Your priority is to stay alive. First work to satisfy your survival priorities of shelter, water, fire, and food. Once you are in a position to satisfy those needs while on the move (such as carrying camping gear or survival items you made) then you can make a plan for navigating out.

Often, the best option is to move downhill until you encounter a stream, river, or other body of flowing water. Water flowing downhill will lead you toward the lowest areas on the landscape, where towns and roads are typically located. If the moving water is in a steep ravine, you can travel along a ridge that is parallel to the waterway.

If you encounter a hilltop, ascend it to survey the landscape for signs of habitation. The glow of lights from cities and towns can be seen from great distances at night. If you can see evidence of human habitation in the distance, you can then navigate your way there. Also, during the day, look for strips of forest that have been cut down to accommodate power lines or roads. Trails or roads under powerlines can be used to travel back to civilization. Also, try to signal passing aircraft (especially helicopters which typically fly lower than planes) with a fire or signal mirror using groups of three. Groups of three are a universal sign for help (dating back to the Morse code signal SOS: three short, three long, three short). So, three fires lit in a triangle, three blasts from an emergency whistle, or three flashes from a signal mirror all mean help.

In Conclusion

When you carry a survival kit that includes a map and compass, utilize the navigation techniques listed above, and have primitive survival skills to fall back on, you will be far less likely to get lost, and you will be prepared for most survival emergencies.

CHAPTER SUMMARY

- Consider your survival priorities (shelter, water, fire, and food) and the "Eleven Systems" when assembling a wilderness survival kit.

- Create separate survival kits for your backpack, car, and home.

- Know how to use each of the items in your survival kits.

- Become familiar with using a compass and topographic map.

- Always carry a map and compass when travelling into the backcountry.

- Practice aidless navigation skills, including paying attention to major landforms (mountains and rivers), recognizing where the four directions are (by noting the position of the sun, moon, and north star), and using trailblazing, songlining, and backtracking techniques when travelling off-trail.

- When planning an outing, always tell someone where you are going and when you expect to be back so that searchers know where to look for you if you do not return. If lost, the best practice is to survive in place so that searchers can find you. If nobody knows where to look for you, or if a week goes by while surviving in place, you will need to navigate your way out while addressing your survival needs.

Afterword

Congratulations! You've come to the end of the book. Now that we've covered the fundamentals of building shelter, purifying water, making fire, finding food, making survival kits, and navigating in the wild, it's time to review the materials, practice the skills, and plan next steps.

KEY CONCEPTS TO REVIEW

PMA and SPEAR

One of the most important survival concepts to remember is to maintain a Positive Mental Attitude (PMA). The brain is the most important survival tool, and it performs best when you are calm, cool, and collected. Use the SPEAR acronym (Stop, Plan, Execute, Assess, and Re-evaluate) to sustain and maintain mental performance while addressing the most important survival needs.

The Rule of Threes and Survival Priorities

Memorize the Rule of Threes: three hours is the approximate survival time without a regulated body temperature before hypothermia becomes a serious threat; three days is the survival time without water before dehydration reaches a dangerous level; and three weeks is the survival time without food before starvation becomes a grave concern.

The Rule of Threes defines the Survival Priorities which are typically addressed in the order of Shelter, Water, Fire, and Food. The order of survival priorities can shift depending on what equipment is at hand or what the environment is. For example, if a tent and sleeping bag are at hand, then water may become the first priority. Or if the environment is cold and rainy, then fire might become the number one priority if it is needed to create a dry and warm shelter.

GET OUT AND PRACTICE

Be sure to get out in the field to practice survival skills. Initial practice should focus on core universal survival techniques: building debris hut shelters; boiling water with hot rocks in coal-burned bowls; making fire from bow drill kits; identifying common wild edible plants; assembling basic survival kits for home, vehicle, and daypack; and navigating with map and compass. One of the best things you can do to move your skillset forward is to find a community or group of enthusiasts who motivate each other, to practice and share knowledge. At first, practice one skill at a time, striving to master each skill separately. Once proficient with each skill on its own, consider going on a survival outing where all the skills can be practiced in combination in a simulated survival scenario. In such a scenario, backup equipment (such as a backpack full of camping gear with a way to contact the outside world in case a true emergency comes up) is essential and can be stashed nearby. This way, a simulated survival situation can be enacted with a safety net in place.

From here, continue your learning journey by adding additional related skills that increase your survival abilities, such as wild plant medicines, wildlife tracking, stone-tool making, primitive archery, basket making, and more. The revered naturalist, Jim Corbett, is quoted as saying, "The book of nature has no beginning, as it has no end"—which means, when it comes to nature and wilderness skills, it is impossible to know it all. There will always be more to learn, experience, and explore.

RECOMMENDED RESOURCES

I hope your wilderness skills journey doesn't stop here. I encourage you to get out in nature and put each of these skills into practice. Build shelters, purify water, make fire from friction, learn to identify edible plants, and most of all have fun while practicing! Many wise elders (and scientists with studies) have recognized that ongoing education is one of the most significant keys to a long, healthy, and fulfilling life! We've listed many books, websites, schools/teachers, and other resources for continued learning in the back of this book. In addition, WildernessCollege.com is a great resource to find additional inspiration, to meet like minds at classes, and to stay connected through our free Alderleaf eNewsletter. If travelling to Alderleaf in the Pacific Northwest is a hindrance or if life is just too busy, we've created an online survival course—*Essential Wilderness Survival Skills* (EWSS)—that is a great companion to this book to support your continued learning. Go to https://www.wildernesscollege.com/essential-wilderness-survival-skills.html to learn more.

THE FUTURE OF WILDERNESS SURVIVAL EDUCATION IS YOURS!

As you now know, everyone benefits from wilderness survival skills. Fortunately, the field of wilderness survival is growing. When I got started in the field there were only a handful of survival schools in the entire country. Now there are many in most states. I hope we will reach a day where there are wilderness schools in every community (similar to the popularity of martial arts schools). And hopefully, at some point in the future, basic survival will even be taught in public schools. In the meantime, there is a great need for individuals to teach wilderness skills and to start new programs. Alderleaf can continue to help you gain more outdoor skills. Our various training opportunities can help you build up your skillset so that you'll be ready to share them with your family and friends and to become a valuable asset to your community.

I hope this book has fed your curiosity, nourished your need to know, and inspired you to get out into the outdoors to learn these essential wilderness survival skills.

Thank you for reading! It would be great if you could leave a review on Amazon. Whether you loved it or not, your feedback is appreciated!

Finally, we have some special survival skill bonuses for you at our website. Get them at:

https://www.wildernesscollege.com/survival-book-bonuses.html

Good luck on your path. We hope to meet you soon at Alderleaf!

Acknowledgments

This book wouldn't have been possible without the support of so many people. First, I'd like to thank all the students that have come through Alderleaf courses since we started in 2006. Your endless enthusiasm, on-point questions, and excellent feedback helped push our curriculum to higher levels.

Next, we are forever grateful to all the amazing core instructors that have taught at Alderleaf Wilderness College (and the many that continue to do so!). Your input helped refine and improve the lessons and instructional materials that have been incorporated into this book. Kudos to Filip Tkaczyk, Heather Swift, Steve Nicolini, Dave Scott, Michelle Peziol, Connor O'Malley, Georgieann Lilgreen, Gabe Garms, Brooke Nelson, Leah Houghton, Bernard van der Weerdt, Chris Byrd, Russell Field, Jeremy Williams, Jedidiah Forsyth, Erika Iverson, and Ben Mardis.

I could not have written this book without standing on the shoulders of giants. We're thankful for the wilderness skills teachers and authors that have come before us. Your wisdom and efforts moved this field forward, providing opportunities for generations ahead.

This book was also a team effort! A huge thank you to Daniel Heila at Best-Ever-Edit and Index for editing and organizing the material. Thank you to Luminare Press for layout, design, marketing, and publishing support.

Importantly, I'd like to thank my family and friends. To my mom and dad for instilling a love for the outdoors. To uncle John for nurturing that interest. To the scout troops and outdoor clubs that provided so much inspiration for wilderness skills. Thanks to my daughter Kaia for all the encouragement. And especially a huge thanks to my wife and Alderleaf co-founder Kerry, who supported me throughout this project, with countless hours and late nights editing and refining this book.

And last, but certainly not least, I'd like to thank you the reader for your interest in wilderness survival and for choosing *The Essential Skills of Wilderness Survival* to expand your knowledge. Hopefully this book has increased your wilderness survival know-how, enhanced your connection to nature, and inspired you to continue pursuing outdoor skills!

Bibliography

Backer, Howard. *Wilderness First Aid: Emergency Care for Remote Locations.* Burlington, MA: Jones and Bartlett Publishers, 2005.

Bohan, Heidi. *People of Cascadia: Pacific Northwest Native American History.* Carnation, WA: Heidi Bohan, 2009.

Elbroch, Mark, and Michael Pewtherer. *Wilderness Survival.* Camden, ME: Ragged Mountain Press, 2006.

Elpel, Thomas. *Participating in Nature: Thomas J. Elpel's Field Guide to Primitive Living Skills.* Pony, MT: HOPS Press, 2002.

Elpel, Thomas. *Botany in a Day.* Pony, MT: HOPS Press, 2006.

Kallas, John. *Edible Wild Plants.* Layton, UT: Gibbs Smith, 2010.

Kochanski, Mors. *Bushcraft.* Auburn, WA: Lone Pine Publishing, 1987.

Mears, Raymond. *The Outdoor Survival Handbook.* New York: St. Martin's Press, 1992.

Newcomb, Lawrence. *Newcomb's Wildflower Guide.* Boston, MA: Little, Brown, and Company, 1989.

Pewtherer, Michael. *Wilderness Survival Handbook: Primitive Skills for Short-Term Survival and Long-Term Comfort.* New York, NY: McGraw-Hill Professional Publishing, 2010.

Pojar, Jim and Andy MacKinnon. *Plants of the Pacific Northwest Coast.* Tukwila, WA: Lone Pine International, 2004.

Schofield, Janice. *Discovering Wild Plants.* Portland, OR: Alaska Northwest Books, 2003.

Tawrell, Paul. *Camping & Wilderness Survival: The Ultimate Outdoors Book.* Green Valley, ON: Paul Tawrell, 1996.

Thayer, Samuel. *The Forager's Harvest: A Guide to Identifying, Harvesting, and Preparing Wild Plants.* Ogema, WI: Forager's Harvest Press, 2006.

Tilford, Gregory. *Edible & Medicinal Plants of the West.* Missoula, MT: Mountain Press, 1997.

Turner, Nancy. *Plant Technology of First Peoples in British Columbia.* Vancouver, BC: University of British Columbia Press, 1999.

Wescott, David. *Primitive Technology: A Book of Earth Skills.* Layton, UT: Gibbs Smith, 1999.

Wescott, David. *Primitive Technology II: Ancestral Skills.* Layton, UT: Gibbs Smith, 2001.

Supplemental Resources

Chapter 1

Outdoor Survival Techniques

Naturalist, tracker, and survival skills teacher Dave Scott tries to answer the unanswerable question often asked of him by students and friends: "How do you live through a full survival situation?"
https://www.wildernesscollege.com/outdoor-survival-techniques.html

Basic Survival Skills

There is so much information on basic survival skills that you might be asking, "Where to start?" Filip Tkaczyk (author of *Tracks & Sign of Reptiles & Amphibians*) provides six primary components of wilderness survival to help you thrive in any situation.
https://www.wildernesscollege.com/basic-survival-skills.html

Outdoor Survival Training

What are the keys to successful outdoor survival training? There are a variety of methods that can be used to learn more about outdoor survival. Here are some great ways to gain more knowledge and experience. Filip Tkaczyk discusses books, videos, training courses, and other resources for growing your survival knowledge.
https://www.wildernesscollege.com/outdoor-survival-training.html

Chapter 2

Basics of Wilderness Survival Shelters

Jason Knight, co-founder of Alderleaf Wilderness College, presents universal principles of survival shelter construction.

https://www.wildernesscollege.com/wilderness-survival-shelters.html

How to Build a Quinzee Snow Shelter

Quinzees are great group shelters to build for fun, though more importantly, they can be built in two shakes of a muskox tail to keep winter backpackers from freezing to death! Steve Nicolini, a former instructor and land steward at Alderleaf, gives the low down on building this snow structure.

https://www.wildernesscollege.com/quinzee.html

Chapter 3

Survival Water Purification (additional information)

Because water makes up more than two thirds of the average person's body weight, it is a vital component of our physiology and even a small amount of water deprivation (also known as dehydration) can be harmful. Jeremy Williams, graduate of the Alderleaf Wilderness Certification Program and former instructor at the college, provides more in-depth information on this essential wilderness survival skill.

https://www.wildernesscollege.com/survival-water-purification.html

How to Make a Primitive Water Filter

Experienced wilderness skills educator and former Alderleaf instructor Connor O'Malley discusses water filtering in wilderness situations. Instructions to make a primitive filter (not effective for removing pathogens) for removing sediment and odor from wild water are presented.

https://www.wildernesscollege.com/make-a-water-filter.html

Giardia Symptoms and Treatment
Filip Tkaczyk discusses the waterborn pathogen Giardia and addresses transmission/infection, symptoms, treatment, and prevention.
https://www.wildernesscollege.com/giardia-symptoms.html

Chapter 4

How to Make a Fire (additional information)
Heather Swift, current ethnobotany instructor at Alderleaf and former ethnobotany instructor at Cascadia Community College, offers some keys to success in learning how to build and start a fire.
https://www.wildernesscollege.com/how-to-make-a-fire.html

Survival Fire Starters
Jeremy Williams discusses several unique and effective survival fire starters from igniters to accelerants.
https://www.wildernesscollege.com/survival-fire-starters.html

How to Build a Fire Pit
Understanding how to build a fire pit with safety and utility in mind is an important wilderness skill. Proper fire pit construction is essential to make the most of your outdoor experiences. Jason Knight presents three important concerns of fire pit construction.
https://www.wildernesscollege.com/building-a-fire-pit.html

Dakota Fire Hole
This unique below ground fire hole is an ancient technique for building efficient, clean burning, and easily concealable fires. Jeremy Williams presents the Dakota Fire Hole technique.
https://www.wildernesscollege.com/dakota-fire-hole.html

Bow Drill Fire in the Pacific Northwest
They say that if you can succeed with a bow drill fire in the winter months in the Pacific Northwest, then you can succeed at it almost anywhere else in the world. Gabe Garms, a graduate of the Alderleaf Wilderness Certi-

fication Program and former Alderleaf instructor, walks you through his dependable technique for starting a fire in damp/wet climates.

https://www.wildernesscollege.com/bow-drill-fire.html

Making Fire with a Hand Drill

Making a hand drill fire is a traditional method used to start fires in dry, low humidity climates. Alderleaf instructor Chris Byrd presents the anatomy, construction, and application of this challenging ancient technique.

https://www.wildernesscollege.com/hand-drill-fire.html

Making Fire with Bow and Drill (additional information)

Of the many ways to make primitive-style friction fires, the bow drill is one of the most practical methods to learn. Filip Tkaczyk presents guidelines for assembling this friction fire-starting kit.

https://www.wildernesscollege.com/bow-and-drill.html

Chapter 5

Plant Identification - A Practical Approach

To effectively identify plants in the field a simple method based on easily observable and comparable characteristics is required. Filip Tkaczyk presents Newcomb's Method of plant identification.

https://www.wildernesscollege.com/plant-identification.html

Wild Edible Plants - Benefits, Hazards, and Major Groups

Filip Tkaczyk discusses important considerations for getting started in working with wild edible plants.

https://www.wildernesscollege.com/wild-edible-plants.html

Wild Edible Greens - Part of Every Meal

Some of the most delicious wild foods are wild edible greens. Filip Tkaczyk presents commonly encountered wild greens and offers suggestions for when to harvest them and how best to include them in your diet.

https://www.wildernesscollege.com/wild-edible-greens.html

Wild Edible Berries

Filip Tkaczyk discusses some details to think about while searching for these wild delicacies.

https://www.wildernesscollege.com/edible-berries.html

Edible Weeds - A Different Perspective

Everywhere we walk, we are surrounded by weeds. This category of plants includes many great edible as well as medicinal species. Filip Tkaczyk introduces edible weeds by looking at what makes a weed, a weed.

https://www.wildernesscollege.com/edible-weeds.html

Edible Wildflowers - Identification, Harvesting, Examples, and Cautions

There are, roughly, twenty thousand different types of flowering plants in North America. In this article, experienced bushcraft instructor Bernard van der Weerdt focuses on several key concepts about edible wildflower species.

https://www.wildernesscollege.com/edible-wildflowers.html

Foraging for Wild Edibles - A Practical Approach

Filip Tkaczyk presents the fundamentals of foraging for wild edibles.

https://www.wildernesscollege.com/foraging-for-wild-edibles.html

Urban Foraging - Eating Your Weeds

Filip Tkaczyk introduces the practice of urban foraging and how it can help benefit you and your family during times of emergency. The truth is many of the weeds we might battle in our gardens and in our lawns are plants that are edible and nutritious.

https://www.wildernesscollege.com/urban-foraging.html

Survival Plants - Essential Survival Tools

Survival plants are found everywhere! Filip Tkaczyk shows how getting to know your local plants can help spice up your lunch and literally save your life! Wild plants can fulfill a wide variety of survival needs.

https://www.wildernesscollege.com/survival-plants.html

Edible Seaweeds

Edible Seaweeds are one of the sensory delights of the living seashore. With their fantastic shapes, colors, and tastes they are quite an experience for the adventurous palate. Filip Tkaczyk explains how they can also be a valuable survival food.

https://www.wildernesscollege.com/edible-seaweeds.html

Edible Wild Mushrooms

Learning about edible mushrooms can seem like an overwhelming process, but don't get discouraged, Filip Tkaczyk takes it a step at a time.

http://www.wildernesscollege.com/edible-wild-mushrooms.html

Primitive Survival Weapons for Acquiring Food

Jason Knight shares information about valuable hunting tools for acquiring food in extended wilderness survival situations.

https://www.wildernesscollege.com/survival-weapons.html

Survival Bow Making Instructions

Learn how to construct an effective bow in a relatively short amount of time. A quickie bow is a fast-made bow for survival situations. Jason Knight shares step-by-step instructions.

https://www.wildernesscollege.com/bow-making-instructions.html

Snares and Traps for Survival Trapping

Knowing how to use snares and traps for survival trapping purposes can help you deal with one of the most challenging pursuits in a longer-term survival situation: the ability to obtain protein. Dave Scott shares survival trapping tips.

https://www.wildernesscollege.com/snares-and-traps-for-survival-trapping.html

Survival Snares: Construction and Use

Survival snares can be an effective way to harvest meat in an emergency survival situation. Former Alderleaf instructor, Steve Nicolini, goes over how to build a basic survival snare.

https://www.wildernesscollege.com/survival-snares.html

Primitive Fishing Techniques

Primitive fishing techniques can be useful skills to know if you find yourself in a survival situation. Connor O'Malley and Steve Nicolini share several tips.

 https://www.wildernesscollege.com/primitive-fishing-techniques.html

Survival Fish Trap

Former Alderleaf instructor, Russell Field, goes over the steps to make a survival fish trap and the how-to of actively using the trap to collect fish.

https://www.wildernesscollege.com/survival-fish-trap.html

Chapter 6

Bug Out Bag - Being Prepared for Emergencies

A bug out bag, or GOOD (get out of Dodge!) bag, is a prepacked bag or backpack that contains essential items for short-term survival in an emergency. Steve Nicolini goes over the essential items of this emergency preparedness tool.

https://www.wildernesscollege.com/bug-out-bag.html

Survival Essentials

In this article, Filip Tkaczyk answers the question, "What matters most?" with regard to wilderness survival.

https://www.wildernesscollege.com/survival-essentials.html

How to Choose a Good Survival Knife

A knife is one of the most potent and versatile tools that you can have with you out in the wilderness. In this article, Jeremy Williams answers the question, "How do you choose the best bushcraft knife?"

https://www.wildernesscollege.com/best-survival-knife.html

How to Sharpen a Knife

One of the most important aspects of knife care is keeping a sharp edge on your blade. A sharp knife is not only more effective as a tool, but is also safer than a dull knife. Chris Byrd presents the whetstone technique of knife sharpening.

https://www.wildernesscollege.com/how-to-sharpen-a-knife.html

Creating a Wilderness First Aid Kit

The wilderness can be an unforgiving place. It is prudent to be prepared. In this article, Connor O'Malley talks about how to put together a good wilderness first aid kit.

https://www.wildernesscollege.com/wilderness-first-aid-kit.html

Top Ten Items for a Survival Kit

Wilderness survival kits can provide you with just the right amount of tools and supplies to make it through a challenging outdoor experience. Jason Knight presents a Top Ten Items list.

https://www.wildernesscollege.com/wilderness-survival-kits.html

Survival Gear List

Not sure what to include on your survival gear list? Filip Tkaczyk presents helpful tips to making it more manageable.

https://www.wildernesscollege.com/survival-gear-list.html

How to Read a Compass

Using a compass is a fundamental way to help you determine your location and direction of travel. Filip Tkaczyk goes over compass reading, a vital outdoor skill.

https://www.wildernesscollege.com/how-to-read-a-compass.html

How to Read a Map

Carrying and knowing how to read a map in the outdoors is an essential wilderness survival skill. Filip Tkaczyk discusses reading the topographic map, one of the most practical maps for traveling in the outdoors.

https://www.wildernesscollege.com/how-to-read-a-map.html

Additional Resources

Alderleaf's Essential Wilderness Survival Skills Online Course: Through inspiring video lessons, Alderleaf instructors bring this book to life by demonstrating each of the techniques covered, showing you how you can further develop your survival skills. It's the perfect companion to this book! Learn more at: https://www.wildernesscollege.com/essential-wilderness-survival-skills.html

Alderleaf's website, WildernessCollege.com, has many wilderness skills resources including videos, classes, and hundreds of how-to articles. Plus, get our bonus resources for readers of this book at: https://www.wildernesscollege.com/survival-book-bonuses.html

Current and Prior Guest Educators at Alderleaf:

CaseyMcFarland.net: Website of professional tracker and author Casey McFarland.

Cohabitats.com: Environmental consultancy guided by the wisdom of nature. Founded by Alderleaf instructor Heather Swift.

EarthNativeSchool.com: Wilderness skills school in Austin, TX, run by former Alderleaf instructor Dave Scott.

HeidiBohan.com: Website of ethnobotanist Heidi Bohan, author of *People of Cascadia*.

KeepingTrack.org: Website of professional tracker Susan Morse.

MarkElbroch.com: Website of professional tracker and author Mark Elbroch.

QuietHeart.org: Wilderness skills classes for kids in Washington State. Founded by Allan Sande.

TerraPhoenixDesign.com: Sustainable living design and permaculture consultants including permaculture teacher Dave Boehnlein, coauthor of *Practical Permaculture*.

ThunderStones.com: Website of expert flintknapper and primitive skills practitioner Dan Stueber.

TrackerCertification.com: Professional-level wildlife tracking certifications. Tracking is a valuable skill for long-term survival situations.

TrackersTrail.com: Website of the professional tracker Nate Harvey.

TrackingSchool.com: Wilderness skills classes based in Virginia, with professional tracker and author Rob Speiden.

VillageLivingSkills.com: Website of wilderness skills instructor Peter Yencken.

WildMedCenter.com: Excellent resource for wilderness first aid training.

More Wilderness Skills Schools, Educators, and Colleagues:

AdventureOut.com: Outdoor skills classes in California.

Apathways.com: Wilderness skills classes in Colorado.

AncestralKnowledge.org: Wilderness skills classes in Maryland.

Bear-Tracker.com: Website of professional tracker Kim Cabrera.

BirdMentor.com: Excellent resource for learning about birding skills that complement survival training.

Boss-inc.com: Wilderness skills classes in Utah.

CarleighFairchild.com: Website of wilderness skills instructor Carleigh Fairchild.

CedarRootSchool.org: Wilderness skills classes in Washington State.

CodyLundin.com: Website of wilderness skills instructor and author Cody Lundin.

CreekStewart.com: Website of wilderness skills instructor and author Creek Stewart.

DavidMoskowitz.net: Website of professional tracker and author David Moskowitz.

EarthBasedInstitute.org: Nature-based coaching and leadership development.

EarthKnack.com: Wilderness skills classes in Colorado.

EarthSkills.com: Wilderness skills classes in California.

EarthTracks.ca: Wilderness skills classes in Ontario, Canada.

EarthwalkNorthwest.com: Wilderness skills classes in Washington State.

EarthworkPrograms.com: Wilderness skills classes in Massachusetts.

FlyingDeerNatureCenter.org: Wilderness skills classes in New York State.

<u>4EEE.org:</u> Wilderness skills classes in northern California.

<u>HawkCircle.com:</u> Wilderness skills classes in upstate New York.

<u>HerbalRemediesAdvice.org:</u> Website of herbalist and author Rosalee de la Foret.

<u>Hollowtop.com:</u> Website of survival teacher and author Thomas Elpel (which includes an extensive list of survival schools across the US and beyond).

<u>Hwos.com:</u> Wilderness skills classes in northern California.

<u>JackMtn.com:</u> Wilderness skills classes in Maine.

<u>JonYoung.online:</u> Website of naturalist educator and author Jon Young.

<u>LeadWithNature.com:</u> Website of naturalist educator and author Dan Gardoqui.

<u>LearningHerbs.com:</u> Excellent resource on wild edible and medicinal plants.

<u>LesStroud.ca:</u> Website of Survivorman, Les Stroud.

<u>LifesongAdventures.com:</u> Wilderness skills classes in Oregon and Texas.

<u>LivingEarthVA.com:</u> Wilderness skills classes in Virginia.

<u>LoveTheEarth.com:</u> Wilderness skills classes in North Carolina.

<u>MattGrahamEarthSkills.com:</u> Website of wilderness skills instructor Matt Graham.

<u>MindfulTracker.com:</u> Website of professional tracker George Leoniak.

<u>NatureTracking.com:</u> Excellent website for learning animal track identification.

<u>NCascades.org:</u> Nature classes in the North Cascades of Washington State.

NicoleApelian.com: Website of wilderness skills instructor and author Nicole Apelian.

NighthawkNaturalistSchool.com: Wilderness skills classes in Oregon.

OnPointTactical.com: Wilderness skills classes for military and law enforcement.

OriginalWisdom.com: Wildlife tracking and guide-training courses.

PhyreDojo.com: Website of survival fire making expert Joe Lau.

PrimalNate.com: Website of wilderness skills instructor and author Nate Summers.

PrimitivePursuits.com: Wilderness skills classes in New York state.

PrimitiveSkills.com: Wilderness skills classes in Maine.

RavensRoots.org: Wilderness skills classes in Washington State.

RayMears.com: Website of wilderness skills instructor and author Ray Mears.

RewildPortland.com: Wilderness skills classes in Oregon.

RootsVT.com: Wilderness skills classes in Vermont.

SchoolofSelf-Reliance.com: Wilderness skills classes in southern California.

SurvivalSchool.com: Wilderness skills classes in Ohio.

SurvivalSchool.us: Wilderness skills classes in Missouri.

TrackersEarth.com: Wilderness skills classes in Oregon and beyond.

TrackingConnection.com: Website of tracking instructor Sophie Mazowita.

TwinEagles.org: Wilderness skills classes in Idaho.

TwoCoyotes.org: Wilderness skills classes in Connecticut.

VermontWildernessSchool.org: Wilderness skills classes in Vermont.

VixCamps.com: Victor Wooten's Center for Music and Nature.

WhitePinePrograms.org: Wilderness skills classes in Maine.

 WholeEarth.org: Wilderness skills classes in Oregon.

WildernessAwareness.org: Wilderness skills classes in Washington State.

WildFoodAdventures.com: Wild edible plants classes in Oregon and beyond.

WildHomesteadLiving.com: Nature-based sustainable homesteading.

WildNatureProject.com: Wilderness skills classes in Indiana.

WildSurvivalSkills.com: Website of wilderness skills instructor Tom McElroy.

WoodlandWays.com: Wilderness skills classes in New York State.

About Jason Knight and Alderleaf Wilderness College

JASON KNIGHT has been teaching wilderness survival skills since 1997. He is a cofounder and lead instructor at Alderleaf Wilderness College. Jason has consulted as a local wilderness skills expert for the Discovery Channel's *Dual Survival* program and has been featured on National Public Radio. He is also a CyberTracker-certified Senior Tracker  and an experienced wildlife biologist that has managed mountain lion studies for the Washington State Department of Fish & Wildlife. Alderleaf Wilderness College is one of the leading outdoor schools in the United States offering training in wilderness survival. With a wealth of knowledge and many combined years of experience, the school's instructors bring a high level of excellence and professionalism to each class. Alderleaf's many courses have included survival trainings for the US Forest Service, the Seattle Mountaineers, and the cast of the award-winning film *Captain Fantastic*. Learn more about Alderleaf at www.WildernessCollege.com

Alderleaf presents...

Essential Wilderness Survival Skills, the online course companion to this book.

Jason Knight and team bring *The Essential Skills of Wilderness Survival* to life by showing you how to implement core survival techniques, from survival shelters and friction fire to water purification and foraging with insightful video lessons and more. Gain additional life-saving skills, a deeper relationship with nature, greater confidence in the outdoors, and valuable resources to share with your family and friends for fun and in emergencies.

Take advantage of our years of experience teaching thousands of students to accelerate your own learning!

Empower yourself today at:

https://www.wildernesscollege.com/essential-wilderness-survival-skills.html